WHAT'S BEST FOR THE CHILDREN?

Resolving the Power Struggle
Between Parents and Children

*Through history when public institutions resisted giving
the people what they wanted, when they resisted peaceful
change, they had it forced on them . . . violently. Indeed,
that is almost the unbroken history of human society.
Public institutions, not meeting the people's needs,
continuing to serve only themselves until violence destroyed
them. After a decade in which the American people saw
and heard more than ever before, it is clear that they are
dissatisfied. But, this time, unlike Louis and history's other
losers, this time we know it! We also know we have the
resources and ability to do what needs to be done, but we
don't know how much time we have!**

* Description from NBC documentary "From Here to the Seventies."
Reprinted by permission of NBC.

WHAT'S BEST
FOR THE CHILDREN?

Resolving the Power Struggle
Between Parents and Teachers

Mario D. Fantini

ANCHOR PRESS / DOUBLEDAY
GARDEN CITY, NEW YORK
1974

Grateful acknowledgment is made for the use of the following: Material from the New York *Times* and portions of the advertisement "Where We Stand" by Albert Shanker. © 1970/71, 1972/73, 1973/74 by The New York Times Company. Reprinted by permission. Excerpt from "A Troubled Opening." Reprinted by permission from *Time*, The Weekly Newsmagazine; Copyright Time Inc. Material from the Associated Press. Reprinted by permission.

Library of Congress Cataloging in Publication Data

Fantini, Mario D
What's best for the children?

1. Public schools—United States. 2. Teachers' unions—United States. I. Title.
LA210.F36   371'.01'0973
ISBN 0-385-00697-7
Library of Congress Catalog Card Number 70-177482

This book is dedicated to:

schoolchildren, their parents and teachers

my own children, Steffan, Todd, Brianne
and Marc and their teachers

my wife, Temmy, a teacher at home

my parents, who were my greatest teachers

CONTENTS

INTRODUCTION

Powerful currents—political, economic, and racial—are converging on our public schools, heralding a storm that will put teacher against parent, to say nothing of the child. To most of us, the storm clouds are not in full view, but it is only a matter of time before they will appear with all their furor. Schools are becoming a battleground. As education becomes more important to the life of families, their demands for better education will follow. A Gallup poll on education conducted in 1973 revealed that over 95 per cent of all public and private school parents felt that education was important to success.[1]

Teachers trying to improve their lowly status are engaged in an intraschool struggle. They appear to be winning important battles inside the schools, but the problem of delivering quality education to a diverse population that needs it still goes largely unattended. Outside threats are now being felt

---

[1] George H. Gallup, "Fifth Annual Gallup Poll of Public Attitudes Toward Education," *Phi Delta Kappan*, Vol. LV, No. 1 (September 1973), p. 44.

by those inside the schools. Teachers are being caught in the middle of a cross fire between internal forces such as school administrators, unruly students, and poor salaries and working conditions and external forces such as community groups, angry parents, and state legislators.

Teachers feel threatened by these forces. As a result of their massive numbers, they have developed strong teachers' organizations to tackle both the internal and the external forces. If they win this combat, they will end up controlling American education. If they lose, they may bring down the schools with them. In either case, the struggle for delivering quality education to an American society that is becoming desperate for it will not be solved.

This book speaks to this collision and recommendations for avoiding it—for the children's sake. They come first.

Our system of public education is basically a nineteenth-century model which simply cannot respond to twentieth- and twenty-first-century needs. This outdated monolithic institution places serious restrictions on the people in it. It is unresponsive to students' distinctive learning styles and culture; limits individual talents and abilities of teachers to deal with the new public demands; thwarts parents' aspirations for quality education for their children; and overburdens taxpayers with high costs and low productivity.

The school as an institution creates an arena in which either frustration or conformity reigns. Those who accept the ground rules generated by the archaic structure find it natural to adjust and defend it. Those who are eager for change find the bureaucracy ponderous. Gradually, this system puts those involved in it in conflict. Allies become enemies, the schools become battlegrounds, war develops. People blame one another for the problems, rather than the system that produces them.

Underpinning this outmoded system of public education is economics. That is to say, regardless of the condition of public education, it is big business, with people vying for control of this multibillion-dollar enterprise. The teachers are the latest group to seek power.

Consequently, in the pages that follow, it would be a serious mistake to think that I am criticizing any of the groups trapped by the system. This is particularly true of teachers and their professional organizations. It would be tragic, indeed, if teachers felt that I was "out to get them." I am trying to show what a dysfunctional system does to people, including teachers. My plea is to get teachers to break out of the "box" imposed by an obsolete structure by joining with students and parents in the remaking of public schools.

If teachers continue to fall victim to the system, then a collision with the public will surely result. This would be tragic for the schools, parents and their children, and the teaching profession itself.

After years as doormats within this outmoded system of public schooling, teachers' organizations have grown strong by carefully organizing new vast numbers until now they are so powerful that they threaten to control the schools. In so doing, they will create a professional monopoly, thereby dangerously eroding the public interest. I repeat: Teacher power is a result of the archaic structure of public education, which is the real culprit in our story.

The irony is that teachers, parents, and students—those closest to the learning front and major colleagues in the quest for human growth—are emerging as enemies, blaming one another and not the outmoded system in a "war" over control of the public schools. The key question for us all remains: Can the victims of institutional outdatedness—i.e., teachers, parents, and students—avoid this harmful collision?

We don't know—the best that we can hope for is for parents, students, and teachers to stop fighting long enough to see that the real enemy is not one group or another, but the structure of the public school itself; that together, they can wield enormous power for constructive reform—updating the schools so that they can be more responsive to the aspirations of each and to the society it serves. How? By developing viable educational alternatives within the framework of public education, teachers, parents, and students can pool their energies on the task of reform rather than battle.

In this story there are no villains—just people responding to conditions not always of their own making. However, priorities need to be established. Therefore, the public must regain its rightful role as trustee of America's most important institutions. Public schools belong to the public—not to professional educators. Despite the problems associated with lay control, a professional elite can only compromise the very purposes of these institutions in a free society. No professional monopoly, however efficient or benevolent, can replace the fundamental principles of citizen review and control.

I offer this book with the hope that teachers and parents can connect as partners in the prodigious task of renewing American education. I present these views, therefore, not as a set of absolutes, but as a possible view to further debate and constructive action among all persons of good will.

I owe a special word of gratitude to my secretary, Sally Abbott, who was always ready to lend a helping hand—and to my family, who provided moral support.

I

PARENT ACCOUNTABILITY AND OUR SCHOOLS:

The Rise of the Educational Consumer

IN THE LAST DECADE the American public has been virtually bombarded with the language of educational reform. That something must change in our schools is an implicit undercurrent of any political discussion, and we have all grown weary with endless descriptions and frantic prescriptions. Out of the unrelenting controversy in recent years, we are left with one accelerating demand: An advanced technological society requires an educated citizenry for survival. Conversely, national, communal, and personal survival in a postindustrial environment requires an appropriate educational experience.

This is not merely an academic exercise, but a raw economic reality. One must accumulate an increasing number of educational credentials to earn a living wage. The growing inability of our existing school system to satisfy even the most superficial needs of a technological society has compelled business and industry to finance their *own* private educational facilities. This growing practice confirms both the overwhelming necessity for education *and* the blatant inadequacy of standard public institutions serving a diverse society.

The effectiveness of a democracy is inextricably bound to the caliber of its schools. Political participation is the product of a sophisticated education, and the cliché of a "literate citizenry" floods the documents of our political history. If a group remains ignorant of its rights in the United States, economic, social, and political possibilities are of little use. Blacks, chicanos, Indians, and other minorities have become particularly sensitive to education as the crucial instrument of their past submergence and future ethnic maturity. If the American school continues to produce functional illiterates among the black, chicano, Puerto Rican, and Indian populations, the movement toward political cohesion is severely crippled. Without mastery of the basic communication and analytic skills, human beings are vulnerable to sophisticated oppression. When suspicions of a systematic conspiracy are articulated by minority group parents, when they accuse the educational establishment of genocide, they are focusing on the essential tool of political reform.

Beyond determining the economic and social potential of our nation's citizens, the school also provides a setting for the psychological development of the individual child. It is the place where he assesses his value as a social and intellectual creature, where he determines the options of his future, where he explores the world around and inside him. Inferior education can and does dwarf the natural emotional evolution of youngsters. In a society that presupposes a respect for human dignity, a competent educational system must seek to nurture individual growth.

Modern education, therefore, should correspond to the needs of the total society, its groups, its individuals, and to the optimal lives of all of these. An archaic educational institution handicaps learners, teachers, administrators, communities, the society at large, and renders us all disadvan-

taged. It is small wonder that the educational consumer—
i.e., parent, student, taxpayer—has retaliated against the public school's failures with an unprecedented militancy. Consider the apocalyptic tone of recent educational literature:
*Death at an Early Age, Our Children Are Dying, The Class-
room Disaster, Crisis in the Classroom, The Atrocity of Education.*

American schools, in their present form, cannot accom-
modate the general and particular demands of the 1970s;
students yearn for relevant curriculum, parents want the
preparatory tools for economic mobility, business and industry require an educated consumer public, professional and lay
social critics want public schools to produce a generation
capable of attacking poverty, crime, drug addiction, racism,
environmental pollution. Although these factors are complicated, they are legitimate concerns of twentieth-century
America, and our schools are not designed to embrace the
nuances of our times.

In his education message of March 3, 1970, President Richard Nixon began by stating, "American education is in urgent
need for reform," thereby establishing the basic public policy
for the decades ahead.

The democratic tradition of institutional reform is through
public accountability. Americans as citizens and consumers
usually rise in protest when institutions lose their connection
to the public. Public accountability in education is at the
heart of the American public school system. The concept of
public is particularly pertinent because it reveals what should
be the basic nature of our major educational institutions—
openness and responsiveness to the citizenry. Under a public
system of education, laymen determine the goals of education
and the policies calculated to achieve them. Professional educators are the specialists to whom responsibility for im-

plementation of these policies is delegated by the laymen. The public then reserves for itself the role of accountant to assess whether these goals are being achieved. The public's right to assess and to hold publicly employed officials responsible is fundamental.

When the educational enterprise is going smoothly, the public does not often exercise its right to evaluate. However, during crisis periods, the public assumes its accountant role. We are in such a period now.

Often, the right of the layman to an account of professional performance is in effect nullified by challenges to his competence to inquire into "professional affairs." However, education is a public, as well as a professional, business. Public education in America was never intended to be a professional monopoly. Through many just struggles, educators, especially teachers, have begun to achieve professional status and protection against political and sectarian denominations. Yet the scales must not tip toward a technocracy (many believe we are well into it already) in which the public, especially parents, cannot exercise the right to examine and help alter the professional process in education.

The concept of lay responsibility can be easily misunderstood. Parents, for example, have the right to make decisions concerning the kinds of programs that best suit their children. Parents can make this type of decision directly; or they can delegate this responsibility to the professional. In either case, it is the parents who make important decisions. Except for the very wealthy, this right is not available to most parents. On the other hand, public responsibility does not suppose that merely to state a requirement creates a binding obligation upon the teacher. There is such a thing as asking too much, and it is true that in a complex system like education, no one element can be responsible for everything that happens. However, the public has a right to expect that its schools will respond to its concerns and aspirations.

It will be the purpose of this section to suggest that the current expression for accountability cannot be met by our present structure of public education. Indeed, we shall try to indicate that this structure handicaps the ability of the professional educator to be responsive except in conventional ways that will increasingly receive public resistance. Especially threatened during this period will be the "frontline" agents—teachers and principals—who will seek protection from their respective professional organizations.

In order to avoid confrontation between the professional educational establishment and the public, a proposal for reform needs to emerge which attempts to protect the rights of the major parties of interest in the process. Such proposals have been hard to come by in the past.

It may be useful to begin with an examination of the major public concerns surrounding the accountability movement today, and then proceed to examine the difficulties public schools have in trying to respond to them.

Before we do, it may serve us well to keep certain largely hidden factors before us. First, we need to realize that of the 206 million Americans, over half are pursuing some kind of education. Nearly 50 million young people are enrolled in our elementary and secondary schools. Another 70 million adults are in some form of continuing education, including college. We are in an educationally oriented society and have, thus far, been willing to pay for this service. What we have is a giant educational enterprise which is second in cost only to defense. Over 40 per cent of our state and local budgets are for education. By 1970 national expenditures for the public schools had reached forty billion dollars.

Education is therefore big business. Whoever is in control

of this massive economic structure wields considerable power. Such a giant economic complex is responsible for a virtual army of workers and utilizes billions of dollars for the purchase of goods and services from a network of commercial and noncommercial firms. Moreover, for millions of parents, sending their children to school means that they have a built-in "child care" service which enables them to work, thus contributing further to the economic picture.

When this vast educational system is open and working, the economic components prosper. However, what happens when this business is closed, when it is not working? Obviously, the economics of education is affected. In our society tinkering with economy can be dangerous. If the users of schools, for example, feel that they are not getting the quality of the services sought, it is possible that they can protest. Certain forms of protest result in closing the schools temporarily. This also means closing off the economics. Or school users may say we are not going to pay as much for the services. Again, the economy is affected.

In one sense, then, education is a marketplace. Those in control of this marketplace can wield considerable influence over who builds the schoolhouses, who sells the books, which banks are used, etc. In another sense, how these moneys are used is of vital concern to the public. After all it is their money, and it is their children who need quality education.

There is, then, a common consideration for all who are connected with the educational enterprise. Who determines how the money is spent? How is the money actually spent? Is it being spent wisely? These questions are raised with all giant business enterprises. We have also come to learn of the shady relationships that have existed between the military and industrial sectors involving single governmental contracts.

Well, it is not impossible that similar dangers can exist in America's second biggest business—education.

How can we make sure that public money is being used solely to help children? What happens when public money does not seem to have the payoff expected by the public? What happens when salaries of professionals get higher as the quality of education gets lower?

In the past the economics of education remained hidden from both parents and teachers. Not so today. School economics, therefore, is a basic political motivator. Money is power. Power can be used in various ways—from helping children to protecting and promoting vested interests. Therefore, in considering the battle for the control of the schools that we shall be discussing, the matter of economics should always be kept in mind.

A second factor that deserves notice, which is also remaining largely hidden, is the effect that the structure of the school has on the people in it. How the school organizes itself, the bureaucratic arrangements, the system of rewards, the attitude toward those being served, the process of instruction, the use of time and place, the norms established, etc., make up an environment that shapes the behavior of those within its boundaries. Thus, for example, if the scholastic institution develops the attitude that it is a privilege to receive the services, then those inside will develop a certain way of thinking about students. If the institutional arrangements call for students to be labeled "slow" or "fast," then the people working with these labeled children will begin to develop attitudes and expectations about the child according to his label. If the school bureaucracy models itself after an industrial factory, then the students will be viewed as proceeding through an "assembly line" with each worker responsible for a specific task. In the end the student ends up a "finished product."

In brief, the school is a miniature society or culture with its own ground rules. All who are within the social system are influenced by it—naturally, almost unconsciously. As an environment, its impact remains hidden from most of us. As a matter of course, people learn the ways of the system and find it normal to behave in ways that sustain the existing operations. Those who want to change this social system find the going rough—the natural tide is to keep the culture going as it is. This is the well-known status quo in education.

Viewing the educational system as an environment that shapes attitudes and behavior helps explain, in part, why certain groups take the positions that they do. Those who are products of this school environment find it natural to see things in a certain way.

However, the mission of the school as an institution is changing. Society is asking it to do many more things than in the past. In fact, the demands are coming so fast that the school cannot adapt itself to comply. If, as some suggest, the structure of today's school is really a remnant of the nineteenth century, then the implications are serious. If schools are nineteenth-century models, then they are designed for an agrarian, not an industrial, society. They were meant to serve the privileged, not the masses.

As new demands emerged, the schools simply added on layers to this basic nineteenth-century structure; e.g., they added a vocational appendage, a special education appendage, an adult education appendage, etc. Also, when we had a major European immigration, we asked the school to acculturate, to assimilate the different ethnic groups. In the name of equality we established a uniform approach to schooling.

The point is that those who are in school today are still operating under this uniform, add-on system of education.

As policies are designed to reform the schools, i.e., to make them responsive to twentieth- and twenty-first-century concerns, those on the inside of the outmoded institution, trying to make it work, are still performing in terms of the dictates of the older, established institutional environment. *It is not their fault because they are doing exactly what the school structure mandates.* However, large sectors of the public are beginning to demand a new responsiveness that can only be achieved through fundamental reform of the institution.

Both the economic and the structural factors are converging silently, invisibly, to facilitate the process of public accountability.

There are at least four overt, interrelated kinds of educational consumer concerns and demands encompassing the current expression of accountability.

In a national climate of public accountability with its focus on increased productivity at the lowest possible costs to the overtaxed citizen, studies of educational effectiveness take on added significance. When massive studies such as those conducted by Coleman[1] and Jenks[2] are interpreted to mean that school makes little difference to educational outcomes, then the taxpayer may begin to pay attention. This in turn can mean that more pressure will be placed on elected officials to cut school costs.

More studies dealing with the basic question "How effective is schooling?" are surfacing. For example, the Rand

[1] James S. Coleman et al., *Equality of Educational Opportunity.* Washington, D.C.: U. S. Government Printing Office, 1966.
[2] Christopher Jenks et al., *Inequality: A Reassessment of Effect of Family and Schooling in America.* New York: Basic Books, 1972.

Corporation has conducted a critical review of the research on school effectiveness for the President's Commission on School Finance. This study concluded much as the others, indicating:

> Finally, the educational practices for which school systems have traditionally been willing to pay a premium do not appear to make a major difference in student outcomes. Teachers' experience and teachers' advanced degrees, the two basic factors that determine salary, are not clearly related to student achievement. Reduction in class size, a favorite high-priority reform in the eyes of many school systems, seems not to be related to student outcomes. In general, the second major implication of the research (and most important one for school finance) is:
>
> > Increasing expenditures on traditional educational practices is not likely to improve educational outcomes substantially.[3]

The third major policy implication of the research is:

> There seem to be opportunities for significant reduction or redirection of educational expenditures without deterioration in educational outcomes.

Obviously, such devastating conclusions run head on into the strategy of teachers' organizations and their request for more money. As powerful as professional organizations are, it is difficult to see how they can oppose an aroused public which is hard pressed to cut costs and which is becoming increasingly convinced that much more money would not improve the schools.

The first set of public demands then is fiscal and deals with the tip of the economic iceberg. Educational costs have reached burdensome proportions for the taxpayer. Faced with an inflationary economy, the overtaxed citizen rebels. Understandably, one of his targets is school costs. School

[3] H. A. Averch et al., *How Effective Is Schooling? A Critical Review and Synthesis of Research Findings* (Rand Corporation, 1972).

finance, dependent as it is on local property tax, is particularly vulnerable. While most parents, for example, place a high value on education, they are trapped into a taxpayers' rebellion against school costs by the local taxing structure itself and by the way in which our public school financing system works. In most of the nineteen hundred school districts in this country, reliance on property tax as the major source of public school funding has finally exploded. Citizen discontent with public schools is in major ways reflective of this property tax dilemma. Problems of the pocketbook turn friends into foes of public schools.

Citizens are now watching the school budget much more closely and are demanding a halt to rising school costs. This new inquiry into public school finance by the educational consumer is proving to be revealing, indeed. Citizens are now raising basic questions concerning specific line items in the budget. In the process, they are questioning long-accepted norms—the idea that lowering class size by one or two students really makes a difference, or having teachers receive automatic salary increments whether or not the children learn. The more parents raise such issues, the more they begin to "catch on" to the hidden economics of education.

Consequently, literally forced by economics to question current fiscal policies in education, growing numbers of public school users are demanding a halt to spiraling educational costs, resisting also formerly "legitimate" school improvement efforts.

Until more equitable school financing policies are achieved to relieve the overdependence on local property taxes as the major source of local support for public schools, the consumer will not likely approve of major increases in budgets. The result will be that public schools will need to see if they can utilize existing resources wisely.

A second set of related demands converges on educational productivity. Tied to the fiscal concerns are those that relate established school practices to educational outcomes. Some citizens put it this way: "Are we getting the most for the dollar?" Others refer to the "relationship between school programs and educational objectives." Obviously, if children are not reading at expected levels, as is the case in many of our urban school districts, parents are asking why. In the past these parents have accepted the verdict that there was something wrong with them, that they were "culturally deprived," "disadvantaged." However, the new mood of accountability has swung attention to the school and its programs. Many parents are now saying, "What is wrong with this school?" They are questioning the leadership patterns, the instructional procedures, the competence of teachers, the institutional arrangements themselves.

Since 1960–61, total school expenditures in the New York City public schools have gone up 200 per cent, while the number of pupils in the system has increased only 16 per cent. The large growth in per capita costs and expenditures reflects surges in personnel and service, substantial jumps in various administrative and support costs, and higher teacher salaries.[4]

In spite of the increased resources that have been directed to educators in New York City, criticism of the city's schools is widespread. Citizens are probably more sensitive about education than any other service they "buy" from the public sector with their tax dollars. They feel that if the basic functions such as education are improperly administered, the

[4] First National Bank, *Profile of a City*. New York: McGraw-Hill, 1972, p. 62.

whole rationale for men to live in organized taxpaying units is called into question.

This mood is not limited to our urban centers, but is growing in suburban areas as well. Many students appear to "turn off" on school. Parents express concern that their children are not motivated. Parents worry about this lack of motivation especially when they can see that their children are able and talented. Parents worry about how their children will ever make college with such negative attitudes toward schooling. Families report students who can read and write, but who are nonetheless deeply disappointed with current school practices. The words "relevance" and "dehumanize" are heard often, and indicate the concern of students and, increasingly, that of parents.

These consumer concerns have reached the policy-makers, the elected officials, who in turn place pressure on state departments of education for improved educational production. The policies, of course, begin to take on strong economic influence. Educational production relates educational input to educational output to achieve increased efficiency in the production of outputs.

Obviously, this is an extremely complicated procedure, easily misunderstood, and a deceptively simple notion for a concerned public to apply quickly for end results. The danger is that simple solutions are attached to complex problems. Public pressure reaches schoolmen who usually respond in terms of the established structure of the school. The response is often viewed as "defensive," giving rise to further misunderstandings between the public and professionals. Nevertheless, we are experiencing only the beginning of educational production demands.

At some levels, educational production is already being

approached by parents and community residents. In New York City, for instance, many parents feel that the principal is the key to increased educational production. In one case— that of P.S. 208 in Brooklyn—parents were engaged in a bitter school boycott over the appointment of a principal. Other urban communities are demanding more black and Puerto Rican candidates for predominantly black and Puerto Rican schools (to counter the institutionalized racism which they feel victimizes black and Puerto Rican students).

In some cases the consumer reaches a stage in which "fraud" or "negligence" is claimed. The landmark suit was filed in Supreme Court of California, November 20, 1972: *Richard W. Doe* (anonymous surname) *vs. San Francisco Unified School District et al.* Filing a complaint in the Superior Court of the state of California, the plaintiff argued that as an eighteen-year-old high school graduate, he had not been taught to read adequately, reading and writing at the fifth-grade level. He contended that his passing through the public schools of San Francisco without being provided the fundamentals of education constituted a case of negligence.

The student seeks $500,000 in general damages and $500,000 in punitive damages and the costs incurred in trying to increase the student's ability to read.

This suit filed with the Superior Court also contends that the state's constitution and education laws and the state and local board are responsible for deficiencies that make him unqualified for any but the most demeaning, unskilled, low-paid jobs.

The suit also charged that the student's mother had been repeatedly assured that he was reading at grade level and needed no special assistance.

This case has attracted national attention, highlighting the increased impetus of parent concern for quality education.

At other levels, educational economists are approaching productivity by examining teacher selection. Consider the following report by Stanford professor Henry Levin:

If one were to attempt to help the school decision-maker spend his money more efficiently, where would we start? An obvious place to begin would appear to be teacher selection, for teachers' salaries represent about 70 percent of current operating expenditures for the elementary and secondary schools. Thus, we might want to ask two questions:

1. Which teachers' characteristics show a relation to a goal that most of us would accept for the schools; that is, student performance on a standardized test of verbal achievement?

2. What does it cost the schools to obtain teachers with different characteristics?

Given answers to these two questions, we wish to ascertain whether we can obtain teachers with more effectiveness per dollar of expenditure. . . .

In terms of relative costs, for a given test score gain for Negroes, it appears that obtaining teachers with higher verbal scores is about one-fifth as costly as obtaining more teacher experience; and the teachers' verbal score route is ten times as efficient as teachers' experience per dollar of expenditure for increasing the verbal scores of white students. The obvious policy implication is that school districts are obtaining too much experience as against verbal proficiency. Accordingly, the schools should try to increase the recruitment and retention of verbally able teachers while paying somewhat less attention to experience. How much trade-off should be made is not evident given our linear results.[5]

The consumer demand for increased educational productivity at efficiency levels of finance will grow during the com-

[5] "Commissioners' Summary of Educational Production Functions and Their Relevance to Education in New York State." Paper prepared for the N.Y.S. Commission on Quality, Cost, and Financing of Elementary and Secondary Education, March 1971, pp. 16–17, 19.

ing decade, placing pressure on those directly responsible to come up with different patterns from those commonly thought to be productive.

The third set of demands in the current call for public accountability concerns consumer participation in educational decision-making. There is a growing sense that professional educators now really control education and that they have been able to achieve a series of decisions being made that have favored professional interests, rather than consumer interest—i.e., students and parents.

There are also studies surfacing that tend to support the conclusion that professionals control the bureaucratic machinery of schooling.[6]

Such perceptions leave important elements of the public with the clear impression that professionals are accountable to no one but themselves. This is leading certain citizens to demand a new governance system for education, one in which the community is closely connected with the internal affairs of the public schools.

While the principle of local control has been basic to American public education, this has been accomplished largely by a central lay school board. However, many feel that a central school board is handicapped by a number of factors, such as the processes of selection, representativeness, dependence on professional bureaucracy, social distance from the grass roots, and small groups deciding for the many.

In certain large, centralized city public school systems, e.g., New York and Detroit, the need for increased participation at the community level has lead to decentralized forms of school governance. However, whether the school district

[6] See, for example, Marilyn Gittell, *Participants and Participation* (New York, Praeger, 1967), and David Rogers, *116 Livingston Street* (New York: Random House, 1968).

is big or small, there is a developing sense of consumer pow-
erlessness vis-à-vis the school as a bureaucratic unit. *Individual* parents express the feeling that their participation is
viewed by schoolmen as a privilege, not a right.

It is understandable that as the educational process grew
in complexity, parents withdrew from internal school matters. Basic educational information became specialized and
almost privileged information for the professional alone.
While this process is understandable, it has also resulted in
a disconnection of the school and community, of the teacher
and parent. In a democracy, information needs to reach the
public if they are to make sensible decisions. Unfortunately,
professionals have not made this information available to the
public partly on the grounds that their technical nature
would not appeal to laymen, partly on the grounds that such
information rightfully belongs within the professional family. Suddenly, many parents awaken to the "crisis in public
education" and try to call for immediate accountability.
However, they are doing so without the benefit of accumulated information and experience, which has eluded them because they have not really been "involved" with their public
schools.

At times, this lack of historical involvement with schools
leads to simplistic demands on teachers, e.g., "You are paid
to teach," "I want my child reading at grade level," "I'm
holding you personally accountable."

Such demands are simplistic because they ignore the fact
that professional talent can be thwarted by an institutionalized system and because there are factors outside the school
in teaching and learning.

Moreover, such simplistic demands lead many professionals
to be skeptical of the right of parents to participate because
of their lack of technical qualifications to engage in educa-

tional decisions. However, the question is actually not whether parents now know how, but what they can come to know through involvement and through open access to educational information.

To be sure, there are many parents themselves who would decide to delegate most educational decision-making to the professional, but even in these cases, parents must be aware that they have made an important decision, that is to say, to delegate responsibility.

Involvement in school affairs is instructional for parents and increases the investment of the home in the welfare of the child in school. Further, parent participation protects the school and the children from purely political and economic influences which may arise if participation is open mainly to other organized groups.

Title I of the Elementary and Secondary Education Act has specific guidelines which mandate parent involvement. For example, on July 1, 1967, the following guideline was in effect:

> *The Title I program includes appropriate activities or services in which parents will be involved.* The applicant should demonstrate that adequate provision has been made in the Title I program for the participation of and special services for the parents of children involved in the programs. The employment of parents in the Title I projects is but one way to implement this provision. The primary goal of such activities and services should be to build the capabilities of the parents to work with the school in a way which supports their children's well-being, growth, and development.

In 1968 the guidelines became even more specific, in suggesting the composition of the local advisory committee:

> *It is suggested* that at least 50 percent of the membership of the committee consist of parents of disadvantaged children attending schools serving the area where projects will be con-

ducted, representatives of the poor from the Community Action Agency and parent members of Head Start Advisory Committee, if there is a Head Start project in the community, and representatives of other neighborhood-based organizations which have a particular interest in the compensatory educational program.

In 1971 federal requirements for parental involvement in Title I specified that each local agency

(1) *shall describe how parents of the children to be served were consulted and involved in the planning of the project* and (2) shall set forth specific plans for the continuing involvement of such parents in the future planning and in the development and operation of the project.

However, the diversity of community cultures converging on the school makes representative forms of participation, e.g., local school boards, less effective than direct *individual* decision-making. It is difficult in a pluralistic society to have a small group *speak for* parents or students. Each parent and student will have to speak for himself. This appears to be the new pattern of participation, especially in something as fundamental as making decisions about one's education.

The fourth set of emergent demands really deals with consumer satisfaction. This may, at first glance, appear to be nothing more than a rehash of the other demands. However, there is a pervasive mood of dissatisfaction with a significant sector of school users, including students, that does not fit clearly with the other types of demands. Certainly, we have heard of a growing loss of confidence in public schools. Teachers' organizations are particularly sensitive to this erosion in public confidence. Here is how one UFT official viewed the "crisis of confidence":

—We also believe strongly that a solution must be found to the basic, urgent problem of the failure of tens of thousands of children to achieve—a failure which has led to a loss of confidence in the profession and has created a great deal of turmoil in many of our school systems. Failure which, too, has led to a proliferation of phony structural changes—like "community control"—filled with empty promises of educational improvement, and to such gimmickry as performance contracting and vouchers.

It is a crisis of confidence to which we, as educators, have contributed somewhat, for we are ever willing—as we should be and as I am doing right now—to talk about our own failures, about the need for educational improvement—but we are often too defensive to say outright that our schools are full of really good teachers, who became good teachers in a trial by fire in the classroom . . . and who are faced very often with the most difficult conditions and least possible supports.

It is a crisis of confidence which has led us into a situation where despite the fact that for the first time in many years we have enough teachers and potential teachers to provide individualized attention to children, to drastically reduce class size—we are told there is a teacher "surplus." There is less and less willingness to spend on education. School budgets are being cut to the bone when additional resources are desperately needed.

More and more, the public feels that anyone can teach; that all you have to do is love children and be able to talk. In part, this too is a result of our success, for we have—thanks to the public school system—a literate and educated public, many of whom feel they can do what teachers do. . . .[7]

Consumer satisfaction also extends to the problem of providing quality education to a *diverse* consumer population. That is to say, we have cultural pluralism as a basic social reality. This diversity in consumer style, perception, and demand is converging on the public school in ways that are quite different from decades past.

At one time, public schools tried to assimilate, acculturate, this diversity into a common mainstream pattern. It is re-

[7] Testimony given by Sandra Feldman on December 13, 1972 on the Proposed Regents' Plan for Changing the Certification of Teachers in New York State.

vealing, however, that this period is past. Diversity is a value that large numbers of citizens want to preserve and cultivate, and not an unfortunate barrier to homogeneity. Yet this diversity results in a range of consumer dissatisfactions today which is really puzzling for the public school. On the one hand, we have different people, parents and students, wanting different things from public schools; on the other hand, we have a public school structure that has been geared to providing a common learning, a common educational process, for a pluralistic society, which most citizens, in fact—perhaps 60 to 70 per cent—still prefer. The mood of dissatisfaction is with the significant number who prefer something else.

We now realize that public schools have expected all students to adjust to the school, rather than the other way around. The school program was imposed on all, sometimes in the name of equality. Yet the call now is for connecting the program with the particular learner, his style, and his cultural group.

A classic case in this effort is *Serna et al. vs. the Portales Municipal School* in New Mexico. In this civil suit the United States District Court ordered the Portales School District to "provide learning opportunities which satisfy the specialized educational needs of its Spanish surname students." The judge's order indicates that this would include "bilingual-bicultural programs and recruiting and hiring more qualified Spanish-speaking teachers and teachers'-aides."[8]

Many educational consumers, especially those who could afford it, have tried to seek satisfaction by sending their children to private schools. Large numbers are now seeking

[8] Judgment, *Judy Serna et al. vs. Portales Municipal Schools et al.*, filed at Albuquerque, July 31, 1973.

satisfaction by expecting more from public schools than they are now getting. This expectation may not be completely related to increased costs of education or to problems of educational productivity, although these are certainly factors. They appear to be related more to the psychosocial concerns of schooling itself. They are much more personalized, dealing with what the school as a social system is, or is not, doing to children. Parents express dissatisfaction with teacher attitude—for example, with how certain teachers relate to children. They are concerned that their children must be exposed to certain teachers who may be "psychologically" damaging to them.

Consumer satisfaction is also gauged by the appeal of such ideas as the "open classroom" or "free schools." Students, in particular, are increasingly vocal about their own lack of rights, the dehumanized nature of schools, the fear of retaliation for any direct criticism of the system, etc. The quest for cultural identity is seen by many consumers as requiring a particularly sensitive school situation.

The basic irony here is that for any expression of dissatisfaction with one set of conditions, there is likely to be an equal number of consumers who express satisfaction with the same conditions. Diversity in consumer wants and aspirations cannot be handled by our largely uniform, across-the-board programs, by expecting the majority to rule, or by forcing everyone into a basic pattern in the name of efficiency or equality. Dealing with this set of demands will be the most elusive, but perhaps the most important.

Of course, there are other strong public concerns. Permissiveness in the schools and busing to achieve racial balance are certainly among the most pressing. However, busing, for example, has already received major attention, and policies have been established on this subject, although tension exists. Obviously, public schools cannot succumb to any public pressure to foster educational practices that are inimical to the values of a democratic society. Exclusivity, whether racial, ethnic, religious, or economic, cannot be imposed upon public schools if these major social institutions are to reflect the noblest values of our society. Consequently, there are public demands in the name of accountability that public schools cannot—indeed, should not—satisfy.

However, our discussion deals more with a new developing relationship between a range of demands of a pluralistic society and how a monolithic public school process can or cannot be responsive.

These dimensions of accountability impose on the professional educator enormous responsibilities which he cannot discharge unless fundamental reform of American education takes place.

Said somewhat differently, if educators respond to this new wave of accountability by calling for compensatory improvements to existing practices rather than constructive reformation of the school itself, then they will be also insuring a virtual collision between the professional and the public, a collision that can only have a devastating effect on the aspirations of each and that of society itself.

I have already emphasized that American educators find themselves inside a public institution that was forged during the nineteenth century. Educators have spent enormous time and energy trying to make this nineteenth-century model of education work for twentieth-century needs. They have developed an elaborate professional establishment in a general attempt to improve the institution. Various professional organizations have been developed to elevate professional standards and promote school improvement. An array of professional meetings have been conducted in an attempt to

develop continuing awareness for encouraging a new effectiveness in learning. Continuous demands have been placed on
the school, which are inexorably connected with the dynamics
of the society itself.

Attempts have been made to respond to public demands.
For example, in the economic demands for labor and industry
in the earlier part of the century, vocational schools were
developed that were not unlike the earlier agricultural schools
that arose during America's agrarian period. During the
space age we saw the schools respond to the need for more
science and mathematics.

Public schools have responded to public demands, e.g.,
special education, adult education, early childhood education,
compensatory education for the economically disadvantaged
population, etc. The public school has been responsive, but
mainly by adding on layers to a basic structure which grew up
in another era and which has controlled the attitudes and
behavior of those within its boundary, especially the teachers.
This add-on strategy for trying to respond to the increasing
demands of society has resulted in a rather expensive and
ponderous system that simply does not have the capacity to
deal with human pluralism. The new accountability is calling
for a more responsive structure in public education itself,
one which is able to deal with the continuous demands for
quality education that flourish in a pluralistic consumer population seeking universal education.

With the help of a $450,000 Ford Foundation grant, an
education law center was established in Newark, New Jersey.
Directed by a law professor at Rutgers, the center will offer
free legal services to the educational consumer, namely students and parents. The education law center will attempt
to utilize litigation as a means of making the schools more
responsive to the diverse needs of the students.

For the most part professionals have proposed improvement efforts to which they are accustomed. Often these proposals are accused of making conditions better for them, rather than for the student. The result seems to be an improved but still outmoded pattern of public schooling.

Now being subjected to a period of economic distress, a diverse society, more than ever before in this century, is demanding increased levels of quality education in various forms and is unwilling and unable to continue to pay for it in the same way that it has in the past. More parents and students, realizing the critical importance of education to their future success, join the protest, placing more pressure on the schools and schoolmen. Professionals, in turn, become defensive, and invariably seek greater protection from their professional organizations.

Ultimately the outmoded structure of our public institutions saves its severest blows for many of the students it was designed to serve. We have spent a decade criticizing the schools for not meeting the needs of our children. It is not necessary to report them here. However, an unresponsive institution breeds alienation. If parents and students do not sense that the school is working for their benefit—do not have the gut-level feeling that they are genuinely welcome in the school, do not believe that this is *their* school—then the psychological implications can be severe. Resentment and hostility lead to reprisals.

Could it be that the growing reports of school vandalism are tied to this negative psychology? If they are, then we are talking about something not only deep-rooted and difficult to erase but expensive. As *Time* magazine reports:

Violence and vandalism have become a bleak, persistent expectation in urban school systems. In Los Angeles, where 66,000 broken windows, arson, and other vandalism cost the school system $2.5 million last year, five German shepherds have been added to the nighttime security patrol. New York City will spend some $5,000,000 this year for alarm systems, closed circuit television and other devices to improve security in its schools.[9]

Furthermore, a school structure that classifies and labels human beings, normalizes status stratification and perpetuates a psychology of self-fulfilling expectations. The school expects more from those classified in certain ways. How does a child feel if the school labels him as a "slow learner" or "underachiever" or "deprived"? In some cases, the procedure used to arrive at a particular label is itself invalid. We are becoming familiar with "test biases." A number of prominent court cases have helped highlight the dangers to human classification in schools. For example:

In Boston, Massachusetts, a suit was brought in 1970 charging that the Boston school system and the Massachusetts State Department of Education, through a faulty method of testing and classification, placed large numbers of children into special classes for the mentally retarded. Damages were sought for each of children allegedly "irreparably harmed" by the classification system.

In California several court decisions and research studies blamed scores on group IG tests for unfair placement on many Black and Chicano Students in special classes.[10]

Public pressure reaches the policy-makers, e.g., state legislators, who begin to consider new accountability legislation that results in budget restrictions for public education, and experimenting with such proposals as "performance contracting" with business and industry for the delivery of educational services at money-back guarantees or "educational vouchers"

[9] *Time*, September 17, 1973, p. 59.
[10] Statewide Testing Legislation and Educational Policy Working Paper #2, by Maureen Webster. Educational Policy Research Center, Syracuse University Research Corporation, Syracuse, New York 13210.

which would give parents the money (for tuition) to choose a school, other than public, if they wish. Such proposals are strongly opposed by organized teacher's groups.

By the fall of 1972 accountability legislation had been enacted in twenty-three states. At least ten other states introduced similar legislation during 1973. Many of these legislative bills focused squarely on efficiency and effectiveness.[11] For example:

California 1972	"to determine the effectiveness of school districts and schools in assisting pupils to master the fundamental educational skills toward which instruction is directed . . . so that the legislature and individual school districts may allocate educational resources in a manner to assure the maximum educational opportunity for all pupils . . ." (Sn 12821, 1972, repealing 1969 version)
Connecticut 1971	"to develop an evaluation and assessment procedure designed to measure objectively the adequacy and efficiency of the educational programs offered by the public schools" (P.A. 665, S.1)
Nebraska 1969	requires the Department of Education to "institute a statewide system of testing to determine the degree of achievement and accomplishment of all the students within the state's school systems, if it determines that such testing would be advisable" (B. 959, 6(d))
Wisconsin 1971	"develop an educational assessment program to measure objectively the adequacy and efficiency of educational programs offered by public schools in this state" (Ch. 125, Laws of 1971, S. 443. 115.28 (10))
Colorado 1971	"institute an accountability program to define and measure quality in education, and this to help the public schools of Colorado to achieve

[11] Ibid.

such quality and to expand the life opportunities and options of students of this state; further, to provide to local school boards assistance in helping their school patrons to determine the relative value of their school program compared to its cost." The program developed is "to measure adequacy and efficiency of the educational programs . . . begin by developing broad goals and specific performance objectives." (Article 41, 123-41-2)

Florida 1968, 1971 — "to provide for the establishment of educational accountability in the public education system of Florida; to assure that education programs operated in the public school of Florida lead to the attainment of established objectives for education programs; and to provide information for an analysis of costs and the differential effectiveness of instructional programs" (H.B. 894, S.2). Assessment is in the context of the 1968 legislation for Educational Renewal, a process whereby goals and objectives of education are continuously modified.

Maryland 1972 — "to provide for the establishment of educational accountability in the public education system of Maryland, to assure that educational programs operated in the public schools of Maryland lead to the attainment of established objectives for education, to provide information for accurate analysis of the costs associated with the public education programs, and to provide information for an analysis of the differential effectiveness of instructional programs. . . ." Requires the State Board of Education to assist local school boards and school systems "in developing and implementing educational goals and objectives for subject areas. . . ." Each school is to establish "project goals and objectives" in line with those of local and state boards. (SB. 166)

These developments create further resistance and resentment by educators, forcing them to consolidate further through their organizations, e.g., the National Education Association and the American Federation of Teachers.

Yet the behavior patterns developed by those inside the public schools are such that they will continue to seek school improvements as they have in the past, which in turn will be unable to satisfy the current public demands.

The structure of the public schools now compels schoolmen to react in three ways. (1) to expect a wide range of school users to adjust to the one standard, rather uniform, public school program. That is to say, schoolmen expect one pattern of schooling to work for everyone. We have developed a vast remedial effort for those who have found it difficult to adjust, and we have a vast classifying system for others such as "slow," "deprived," etc.; (2) to expect a more-of-the-same approach to educational improvement. For instance, we believe that if children cannot read, we need more remedial reading teachers. If children are "turned off," we need more support staff (counselors, psychologists) to turn them back on. If individualization of instruction is important to learning, then the best, most stable route is by lowering class size—i.e., add more teachers. This add-on psychology (without different utilization of existing resources) is inefficient and costly and runs head on into public disapproval; (3) to engage in an internal political battle among professionals: school administrators versus teachers—management versus labor. Teachers, long considered the doormats of the system, have formed very powerful teachers' organizations in order to demand better salaries and working conditions.

These new internal power arrangements do not lead to reform but further "freeze" existing practices, i.e., those that are acceptable to their constituents: teachers and administrators. These kinds of orientations make it extremely difficult to deal with the new public accountability.

Teachers are especially constrained by this structure. Put into egg-crate classrooms in which they close the door to work with twenty-five or thirty-five children, often more, teachers, not having been prepared to teach for cultural pluralism or deal with the wide range of different learning styles that converge on them, attempt merely to survive. Really learning to teach on the job, teachers develop their own teaching style in the process. Further, they find it very natural to simply impose their learning style on a group of youngsters. The youngsters who do not respond to the teacher's style are viewed as problems. Obviously, no parent likes to hear that there is something wrong with his or her child, and conflict results. Further, if at the request of a parent the principal attempts to move the student from one room to another, severe internal problems result. The teacher might "lose face" if he or she felt that the principal was supporting the student and not the teacher. Such episodes reach the other teachers and teachers' organizations. The principal then becomes suspect, co-operation is undermined, etc. Under present conditions, if parents come in and make demands about changing the child's teacher because of a personality conflict, the teacher in that situation watches closely to see whether the principal goes on the side of the teacher or the student. Because teachers are more "powerful" politically than students or parents, many students are forced into situations not conducive to their growth and development. Over time, the cumulative effect of this type of policy is to turn parents and community against school and teacher.

Moreover, teachers' organizations, dependent on teacher satisfaction for their own existence, must protect their members. These protections become contractual through negotiations: such items as salaries, hours of work, kinds of work, seniority, tenure, have been supplemented by class size (pupil-teacher ratio), and disruptive children (teacher determines which children remain in her classroom), etc.

These hard-won items tend to freeze the teacher into an acceptable mold of operation. They become the standards by which quality education is measured. They all make sense if the mission is to make a uniform pattern of education better, but they may have little to do with real reform of public schools or with the range of complex demands emanating from a diverse consumer population.

Further, the school administration (superintendent, principal), once the major source of authority, has witnessed a steady relinquishment of this power to organized teachers. This loss of real authority does place the principal in a difficult position during this period of accountability. He appears to be the official most likely to be held accountable for the quality of educational services being delivered. Consumers, parents and students alike, go to him with their concerns. However, he is caught between increased teacher power on the one hand and growing consumer discontent on the other. His own power limited, he finds it difficult to implement basic reform without threatening established teacher interests and/or his own security.

Parent- and community-oriented groups are quickly picking up the implications of teacher contracts which begin to reveal how building principals are actually accountable to teachers. For instance, in the New York City teacher contract, guidelines for school safety call for principals to be accountable to teachers for safety in the schools. The Committee for Community Schools, a community-oriented organization, responded to this feature of the teacher contract by questioning: "Who is accountable to the parents and students for the quality of education?"[12] The publication of the Committee of Community Schools, *The Worksheet*, is widely distributed.

The principal, as chief accountability officer, needs to be the orchestrator of a multitude of resources, human and material. This orchestration is intended to maximize learning for all students, thereby insuring consumer satisfaction. If the administrator, school principal, or superintendent, for that matter, is clearly in a position where he is unable to orchestrate and is still held accountable, then he is placed in an untenable position.

Obviously, it is difficult to hold teachers accountable as individuals. How can the public hold teachers accountable? They are like individual players of an orchestra or a football team. It is the orchestrator of the total effort who is given this responsibility. It is the school that is the basic unit of accountability, yet the teachers collectively have much of the "power" to generate reform. Obviously, new relationships between parents and teachers must emerge.

Further, when heads of teachers' organizations are asked how teachers are going to be held accountable, the answer is usually along the lines, "We will gladly be held accountable for all those things we have control over. Since we have no control over the socioeconomic level of students or have not selected the principal, we cannot be held accountable."

We have an ironic situation in which teachers collectively have power, but individually they cannot really be held accountable. Public accountability still faces the administrator. In big city school districts the vulnerability of the school su-

---

[12] Committee of Community Schools, *The Worksheet*, Vol. 2, No. 1 (September–October 1972).

perintendency is particularly obvious. His power eroded; the superintendent is made a scapegoat for inaction. The public, demanding quality, still holds the superintendent accountable, thinking he has reign over the implementation of school policy.

Boards of education—the trustees of public schools—have tried to be the determiners of policy. School administrators have been the executors of these policies. However, this process has been significantly altered by the internal politics of public education taking place over the past decade.

Many school districts have a "balance of power" political arrangement in which school boards, school administrators, and teachers' organizations all share authority. While this may appear desirable on the surface, such alignments also have a "checkmate" effect on school reform—to say nothing of the havoc they play with public accountability. Especially during times of reform is such a split in authority and responsibility confusing. The public, for the most part, still perceives the central school board and the superintendent of schools as possessing the most authority and, in turn, responsibility—and thus as accountable for school improvement efforts. *But teachers' unions also have power. Yet teachers' unions are not subjected to the same public accountability. As professional organizations, they are at the same time inside and outside the system of public education.* As professional entities, the public has little right of review of their activities. On the other hand, as the collective bargaining agents, they influence school affairs very directly. They can determine when a teacher will work, and often with what children. They determine how many children will be in a classroom. They determine how many times a year a principal will supervise the teacher, what type of program will be offered, etc. Ironically, the most powerful figure in the public schools may be the president of the teachers' union, and he is beyond public accountability.

This gradual infringement on matters of educational policy has gone relatively unnoticed by the general public—especially the frustrated consumers who still make their demands felt to school boards which, in turn, place pressure on the superintendent of schools, who is trapped by the existing system of power politics. Especially in big city school systems have the results of this political process been most evident. The term of office for many urban superintendents is just about two years—hardly enough time to deal with the basic problem of school reform.

Yet this political arena forces school boards, which themselves are experiencing an erosion of their policy-making authority, to pressure the chief school administrator—as if he could somehow salvage the ball game. When he cannot, the board fires the superintendent and hires a new one, thereby giving the public the impression that they are still on top of things. But the new superintendent cannot bring about reform, because to do so would mean running against prevailing interests and negotiated agreements of teachers.

If the superintendent does nothing, then public pressure is unleashed on the school board, which must respond. Again they look to the superintendent, who becomes the fall guy.

School boards can fire superintendents, but they cannot fire the president of a teachers' union. Further, teachers can bring the entire system of public education to a halt by striking. Consequently, if the board attempted to deal with teacher power, it would run the risk of stopping education for the public.

It simply is easier to deal with school administrators. If they were fired, the schools would still run. Teachers can bring schools to a halt—but so can parents and students. These are the consumers themselves. We have seen occasions in which both parent power and student power have brought schools to a halt. The politics of education will doubtless see the power arena expanded to include a balance of power among school boards, school administrators, teachers, parents, and students. As the demands for quality education continue, so will the tug-of-war. Initially, the teachers will maintain an upper hand, by virtue of their superior organizations, but gradually the public, led by the consumer, will reclaim this power.

In the meantime this tug-of-war of authority between teachers' organizations and school boards and school administration is occurring throughout the public school systems of the nation. The issues in negotiation are clear-cut on both sides as this report from a school system in New York State exemplifies:

> Representatives of the teachers' association and the district administration thus far have spent some 60 hours at 12 different sessions haggling with each other over next school year's teaching contract. The present two-year agreement expires June 30.
>
> An Association memorandum outlining the contract proposals of the two sides was obtained by The Times-Union yesterday at a teachers' meeting.
>
> According to the memo, the teachers' contract proposals include:
>
> A NEW "PROFESSIONAL AUTONOMY" clause that would give teachers more of a say in the educational administration of the schools. Under this clause, a chief-of-staff, team leaders and curriculum specialists would be elected by the teachers at each school. The teachers also would have veto power over any decision to hire a new teacher.
>
> LETTING ELEMENTARY STUDENTS out of school at 1:30 P.M. every other Friday so that teachers have time for team planning activities.

MAINTAINING THE PRESENT 27.5 to 1 pupil-teacher ratio, and setting the upper ratio of each class at 32 to 1. Some classes now have as many as 42 students.

A FRINGE BENEFIT PACKAGE that includes payment of all dental work and nearly all medical bills.

According to the memo, the district's proposals include:

GIVING EACH PRINCIPAL the authority to set educational goals for teachers and then evaluating them on the basis of achieving those goals.

REQUIRING A TEACHER to stay after school at the request of the principal, a parent or a student.

DELETING THE STAFFING RATIO, thus permitting an increase in class size.

INCREASING THE WORK YEAR to 186 days by cutting the February recess to two days.

ALLOWING THE ADMINISTRATION to transfer teachers from building to building without permission.[13]

In the meantime, the problems of reform will be fraught with difficulty. The teachers will find it natural to play by the ground rules of the existing structure. They will deal with school improvement mainly through add-on measures that are least threatening to them and easiest to implement. These compensatory efforts will cost much more money—something the public is increasingly resisting. Thus, another basis for confrontation between public and professional is carefully laid.

These new internal political realities will necessitate a new style of administrative leadership based on shared authority. Administrators will need to help staff identify problems facing the school, provide all pertinent information to the staff so that alternative approaches to the problem may be planned, with likely consequences, on a co-operative basis.

The point is again made: Our present institutional ar-

[13] Rochester *Times Union*, March 14, 1974.

rangements govern professional behavior. We have developed operational norms which may make good sense to those inside the schools, but which are increasingly being challenged by those outside. Professionals want to be responsive to the various public demands, but find that they can only respond in ways that are unacceptable to large numbers of public school users.

Thus, if parents want increased individual attention given to children, then professionals respond by indicating that they cannot individualize without significantly lowering class size for all teachers, an approach that runs counter to taxpayer sentiment at this time.

Similarly, professionals agree with many communities that schools serving the poor, mostly minorities, are not educating children. Professional response is compensatory education, which is a more-of-the-same approach, but in more concentrated form. Yet President Nixon, in his education message of 1970, reports, ". . . the best available evidence indicates that most of the compensatory programs have not measurably helped poor children to catch up. . . ."[14]

Of enormous importance is the fact that the current public school arrangements restrict the talents of professionals who want to move in new directions. Teachers who express an interest in new forms of education, e.g., open classroom and schools without walls, come directly into conflict with established norms. They may, for example, be ostracized by their peers for being mavericks, or they may be expected to prove that their proposal will work when it has never been tried.

Moreover, the politics of public education has now created a stage on which so-called reform proposals will be scrutinized

[14] 91st Cong., 2d sess., Document No. 91-267, House of Representatives, March 3, 1970, p. 5.

in terms of vested interests. Any proposal that questions established norms is immediately suspect and therefore becomes the object of widespread professional criticism. We have witnessed this with virtually every major reform proposal —desegregation, decentralization, vouchers, performance contracting.

It is vitally important for us to understand that all these behaviors are quite reasonable and proper given the present framework of public education. Once again we must emphasize that the environment of the public schools compels these types of responses from those inside the institutions trying to make them work.

Professionals are often right when they exclaim, "Parents don't understand our problems." How can they? Parents do not "live" inside the school. In fact, as we have suggested, many parents have been apart from the internal current of education for some time. This has been part of the problem. We cannot expect parents and other citizens to know what they have not experienced.

The fundamental concern, of course, is that the drama which is unfolding among the basic parties at interest— teachers, parents, and students—is likely to culminate in a "we-they" type of political confrontation. If professionals, "trapped" by the same system that restricts the consumer, cannot break out of the cycle, then at a time when quality education is crucial to consumer survival, we will witness a major political confrontation. Professionals will win a few battles, but will they "lose" the war?

While the American public has gone to considerable pain to remove external politics from education, it ironically ends up having relinquished the schools to the internal politicians —professionals in general and teachers' unions in particular. Concerned as it was with the effect that the external clubhouse politics would have on education, the public demanded that the organization, personnel, and financing of education be separated from the general operation of city government.

Civil service examinations, credentialing procedures, and complex regulations were preferable to the patronage system that penetrated the pre–World War II system of public education. Still, they created problems of their own. Not only were they depriving the poor and immigrant city population from a chance for employment (how could they meet the new requirements for entry into the profession?) but also they were helping to create a system in which professionals on the inside, through intricate civil service requirements, were protected from outsiders—the consumers—that they were to serve.

This move to separate established politics for public schools was taking place at the very time educators were trying to improve their professional status. Educators, cognizant of the importance of their roles—they were, after all, shaping the hearts and minds of succeeding generations—resented the low status accorded them by society. Envious of doctors, dentists, and lawyers, schoolmen frantically fought to emphasize professionalism. They tried frantically to emulate the medical profession.

They pointed to the control that the medical profession had over medicine. The American Medical Association was viewed with awe. This professional body could challenge governments, protect its members from an uninformed public, control entry into the profession, police its ranks, etc. Through the efforts of the AMA, the status of doctors in America had increased and they had become affluent.

Somehow doctors seemed to generate a collective mystique. They seemed to stick together under the framework of a strong AMA.

Educators, on the other hand, were subjected to lay scrutiny. Laymen told educators what to teach. Lay school boards controlled the schools, not the professional educators who had spent long years in formal preparation—just like doctors. If doctors could control medicine, why shouldn't educators control education? This logic is music to the ears of schoolmen.

As the credentialing process grew, occasioned by reforms which separated schools from local government, so did the thrust toward professionalism among educators. School administrators formed strong professional organizations such as the American Association of School Administrators. Thousands of administrators assembled in Atlantic City at their annual conference, which attracted national figures, including presidents and vice-presidents of the United States.

The National Education Association, until recently composed of administrators, supervisors, and teachers, became the closest thing to the AMA. Concerted efforts to increase memberships resulted in a membership of over two million in 1972.

Professionalism was spending within a system of public schooling that was becoming increasingly centralized and bureaucratized. Each school district had a "central office" which housed the chief school administrator and his supervisory staff. This "central office" represented the "power" base of the school system. Most decisions were made in this central office. Clear "line and staff" functions were established. The flow of decision-making proceeded from the top down. This authority hierarchy proceeded from superintendent down to teacher, who was low man on the bureaucratic totem pole.

Rules and regulations emanating from central headquarters proceeded down to the individual schools.

School boards, representing the public interest and lay

trustees of the schools, had periodic meetings with the central staff to review school policy. However, as matters of education became more complicated—this enhanced by professionalism —school boards delegated increased authority to school superintendents. Some superintendents kept school boards occupied with enormous packets of information too voluminous for any working layman to peruse. Laymen, denied access to information now considered to be "privileged professional information," became preoccupied with the amount of pencils, paper clips, and toilet paper used.

Many school boards were kept so busy dealing with details that they hardly got to policy matters. Instead, the superintendent began to assume more responsibility for policy formation and implementation. Overwhelmed by professional behavior, many laymen accepted the recommendations of the superintendent on matters of personnel, finance, and curriculum.

Centralized decision-making has certain advantages. It is efficient. Parents and other citizens knew to whom to complain. Since the superintendent was the key decision-maker, he became the "court of highest appeal."

Below the superintendent in power was the building principal. As chief administrator of the individual public school, the principal appointed by the superintendent was loyal to him. He had almost complete control of the school, including the teachers. A principal determined which teachers would remain and which would be terminated. He evaluated all personnel in the school. Such authority made teachers particularly vulnerable. Many had to "cater" to the whims of principals or face the threat of job loss.

Parents, knowing the authority of the principal, could go to him for direct action. Yet many parents, like teachers, feared the principal. He was the most educated, the most "professional," official in the building. He could overwhelm the laymen with "professional" rhetoric. Too, many parents, feeling that the education of their children was a privilege, not a right, hesitated to challenge him.

This hierarchical structure posed severe internal problems among educators themselves. Teachers closest to the learner were furthest from decision-making. Furthermore, there were more teachers than administrators, yet they seemed to be the weakest link in the system. While everyone spoke of the importance of teachers, this status was not reflected in the organization itself.

As teachers began to request a decent salary, they realized that this was largely a matter determined by the central office and school board. Further, any increases were subjected to the evaluation of the principal. Teachers who became too outspoken became suspect. The principal could "make things rough" for him.

Slowly, teachers began to organize out of necessity. They were the underdogs of a bureaucratized hierarchy. They had no place to go but up. The political process of gaining improved status within the bureaucracy inevitably unleashed the full potential of teacher power. If teachers could unify around their common plight, they could become a potent political force. They could make demands under threat of doing what no other professional group in the school system could—bring the schools to a halt.

These internal politics went largely unnoticed to a public already being shut out of the schools through professionalism. By and large, the public still carries around the image of the teacher as a quiet spinster, committed more to children than to the worldly things of life, and as a poor underdog held in check by an all-powerful school administration.

Although today many parents have awakened from their

isolation, it will take some time to alter the old image of teachers. Parents still believe that the authority resides with the superintendent of schools and/or the building principal. Their long slumber has made them miss the many hard political battles taking place within the profession itself— battles that are still being waged and that have seen the emergence of the *collective* teacher as the most powerful agent in the school.

The basic difference between the *individual* and *collective* teacher is crucial. As a professional educator the teacher is an independent agent, committed to use his or her specialized pedagogical expertise to enhance the growth and development of all learners. In this individual professional role, the teacher can make independent judgments concerning the various ways of enhancing the learning environment of children. In this capacity the teacher is a "child advocate." That is to say, he gives highest priority to the learner and has a professional duty to do all he can to enhance the learner's potential for growth.

The teacher as an individual, for instance, can make decisions concerning the length of his working day, the methods and procedures for his teaching, and a score of other personal policies which he will use to improve learning for children. In short, he is his own "professional man."

The collective teacher *delegates* many of his individual professional rights to a professional organization. He agrees to support the priorities established by the majority of teachers in the organization. The collective teacher agrees to give priority to the interests and welfare of teachers. He agrees to subjugate his own independent judgments on behalf of the professional group, and its representatives.

The collective teacher is being fostered by the professional unionization movement now taking place in education.

"What's best for teachers" becomes the group norm. Those teachers who attempt to express independent professional judgments that run counter to this collective value tend to be subjugated to group pressure. Loyal teachers are those who follow union policies. This may mean joining colleagues on picket lines, co-operation in job actions, assuming a resistance stance vis-à-vis certain programs or policies, etc.

Union power is derived from collective strength. Any weak links in the power chain are risky.

It must be underscored again that the move from individual to collective professional teacher has been in large measure caused by repressive policies governing teachers' wages and working conditions established by the administrative sectors of the public education establishment. In order to gain decent wages and working conditions, teachers had to unite. In the process of uniting, the individuality of the teacher became eroded.

The implications of all this for schools are considerable. For one thing the entire relationship of educational administration to teachers has been drastically altered. The building principal, at one time, was the leader of the entire professional staff. He represented teachers in professional matters. In fact, he dealt with teachers as individuals or as the staff of his school; now he must deal with them as members in a union. Since teachers cannot easily make independent judgments and are bound by the agreements established by collective bargaining, the principal increasingly must negotiate with the building "rep" (the elected teachers' union representative).

Consequently, as collective teachers give priority to their own welfare, they give lower priority to the welfare of students. Increasingly, the building principal as a decision-maker is placed in a dilemma of siding with either the teachers and their union or the students and their parents.

The president of the New York State United Teachers makes clear the fundamental difference between individual teacher and collective teacher and why the latter is embraced by his teachers' organization:

> . . . Because teachers are wary of the "influence game" being played with them by administrators and outsiders, because they see their power base residing in teachers speaking collectively, and because the significant improvements in their professional status have been a result of their locally negotiated contracts, they recognize that teacher participation does not mean the participation of an individual teacher, but the significant involvement of the teachers they have elected to represent them.
>
> This concept seems to be obscure to many. I was asked to present the viewpoint of the *teachers' organization* at the conference, while yet another teacher was asked to present the "teachers'" point of view on consortium governance. Can individual teachers express anything but their individual ideas, biases, or suggestions? When individual teachers agree with other parties in a consortium can they agree for anyone but themselves? The obvious answer to these questions is "no."
>
> The obvious truth is that if teachers are not represented in consortium via their local teachers' organization, the voice of teachers is not being heard and one of the most powerful groups in the educational community is being disregarded . . .[15]

This administrative shift is particularly noticeable at the superintendent of schools level. Increasingly, the chief school officer, especially in larger school districts, is finding his own authority being stripped through union contracts. *He is no longer the chief leader of all professionals in the district.* He is management and teachers are labor. The professionals are divided clearly into these two opposing camps. He does not—indeed, cannot—speak for teachers; only the union leaders can do that. Increasingly, the superintendent of schools is being forced to choose between teachers and students, the

[15] *The New York Teacher*, February 24, 1974.

organized profession and the public. Increasingly, the superintendent is having to consider becoming a child advocate and protector of the public interest. Assuming such a role places the administrator in direct opposition to the teachers. However, without teacher support no real educational improvement is possible. If collective teachers choose to resist the educational direction being proposed by the chief administrator, there is little anyone can do about it. The superintendent who chooses to "take on" the collective teacher is placed in an untenable position.

While he may receive some public support, his job is to get results. There is no way he can fire all the teachers or assume a no-compromise policy with the teachers' union leaders. To survive he is forced to compromise. This compromise may be in terms of what is best for children. If he does not compromise, he invites great teacher resistance and continued nonimprovement. It is only a matter of time before the public will place pressure on the school board for results. The school board, in turn, will inevitably be forced to seek a new superintendent, this time perhaps someone who is more acceptable to the teachers' union. This can only mean that the new person will be assuming a more sympathetic attitude toward the agent of the collective teacher. Gradually power and control are ultimately transferred to the unified teachers.

The collective teacher can become a national body. One of the prominent leaders in the movement to organize teachers into a national union makes this agenda item clear:

But teachers have also come to realize that their own jurisdictional struggles make as little sense, and that the only intelligent way to combat the dangers facing them is to stop wasting their energy and money fighting each other. The movement toward unity was given a powerful stimulus last week, with the founding of the United Teachers of New York, a statewide teachers union. If this new state group succeeds in uniting the 250,000 teachers in New York State, it could well mark the beginning of the organization of the largest and most powerful group in the nation—3,000,000 educators. The triumph of this effort would have an impact even more profound than that of the collective bargaining revolution in education which began a decade ago.[16]

The end result of all this accountability is that parents and teachers, long allies in the crucial job of teaching the young, are on a collision course. This may seem like a drastic conclusion. It is! How can this be? The words "parents" and "teachers" are almost inseparable. Parent Teacher Associations is a household phrase. To be sure, we have begun to joke about the PTA with its "cookie sale" image, but even so, the friendly relationship of parents and teachers is always assumed.

After all, parents entrust their children to teachers. *In loco parentis*—one of the foundations of public education—means the teacher is a substitute parent. Parent and teacher are welded by a common interest in the child. How can anything come between such natural partners? The wedge being forced between them goes beyond the shattering of a long-standing partnership and toward confrontation. Slowly, the "T" in PTA is being dropped in America's largest city, where the United Parent Association (UPA) represents over 400,000 members. UPA views itself as a parents' union.

A household publication like *Changing Times* carries a piece entitled "Look How the PTA Is Changing," pointing out the new direction of this nine-million-member organization toward greater activities in school affairs.

The movement toward increased citizen participation in education has led to the development of several prominent

[16] "Where We Stand," New York *Times*, October 31, 1971.

consumer-oriented organizations. For example, the National
Committee for Support of the Public Schools in Columbia,
Maryland, is dedicated to furthering of a citizens' lobby for
public education. In announcing the directions of the citizens'
lobby, the National Committee stated:

> The Committee plans to seek a large membership and to
> help activate groups of citizens interested in reforming and
> strengthening the public schools.
>
> The major mission of the Committee will be to greatly
> increase active participation of the public—parents, citizens
> and learners—in the educational decisions that affect them at
> the local, state and national levels.
>
> The Committee's membership and fund raising will begin
> this fall. However, to begin operations, the Committee an-
> nounced a $450,000 grant from the Ford Foundation.
>
> With this generous support, the National Committee is
> pleased to announce that Dr. Carl L. Marburger, former Com-
> missioner of Education for the State of New Jersey; Dr. Wil-
> liam Rioux, President of the Merrill Palmer Institute in De-
> troit; and Mr. Stanley Salett, former Assistant Commissioner in
> the State Department of Education in New Jersey will assume
> the staff leadership of the National Committee.[17]

The Committee further stated why a citizens' initiative was
needed in education:

> Questions may be raised as to why a citizens' organization in ed-
> ucation is needed at this time. The need for an organization to
> protect and promote the public interest in education is more
> acute today than it has ever been before. In a democracy which
> is steeped in tradition of public control of public education,
> there are dangerous signs of extensive erosion. Notwithstanding
> the citizen voice in election of school board members, the
> serious problems of power and control being waged within
> education are unfortunately not always in the best interests of

[17] National Committee for Support of the Public Schools, undated
news release.

children. Private associations of teachers, for example, eschew suggestions that the effectiveness of their members should be subjected to evaluation. . . .[18]

At Yale University, Don Davies, former Deputy Commissioner of Education in the United States Office of Education, helped form the Institute for Responsive Education. This non-profit organization was created "to study and assist the process of citizen participation in education." A publication of the Institute, *Citizen Action in Education*, makes its case for parents' and other lay citizens' involvement in public school reform.

> The grumblings are loud and clear in the swirling world of public education: school systems have become overly centralized and bureaucratic, excessively professionalized, and unresponsive to the changing social needs. Many people seem to sense that they are paying too much and getting too little. . . . School boards and the central administration staffs and teacher organizations too often seem to be a force against change rather than for it. Many teachers and administrators feel trapped in a change-resistant system. And the parents and citizens . . . Yes, there lies the main hope for educational change—in the citizens, parents, students, employers emerging as a "third force" to overcome the inertia of school bureaucracies and teacher organizations. Much in the same way they occasionally have overcome other problems by becoming more active, more vocal, more informed, and more demonstrative on community and national issues. . . .[19]

In professional education circles, the notion of unionization does raise the dual concerns of loss of individual freedom and dividing the professional ranks between management and labor. Moreover, these issues apply also to higher

[18] Ibid.
[19] *Citizen Action in Education*, Institute for Responsive Education, Volume 1, No. 1, winter 1974.

education. For instance, the matter of faculty unionization was considered at New York University (NYU) in the
winter of 1973. In a letter to the faculty, NYU president
James Hester focused squarely on the dual concerns when he
wrote:

> Unionization would introduce rigidifying formalities that would
> hamper the individuality of the separate faculties and restrict
> the freedom of action of each faculty member.
> Unionization would do violence to an effective relationship
> among faculty, librarians, administration, and trustees developed
> cooperatively over many years, and would substitute an alien
> adversary structure which would only lower the status of faculty
> and librarians as professionals and damage their dignified and
> effective role in the university.[20]

The trend toward national teacher merger solicited strong
reaction from some of the educational consumer-oriented
groups. For example, People Against Racism in Education
(PARE), a multicultural organization of parents, students,
teachers, and other members of the school community, carried
a long article (in their journal) called "Ultimate Teacher
Power—N.E.A.-U.F.T. Super Union." Among the concerns
expressed in this piece was the following question:

> . . . Will a combined NEA-AFT create an organization geared
> and dedicated to educating kids or to amassing political power
> in the service of narrow self-interest?[21]

The article went on to consider:

> Beyond the question of the general unionist vs. professional
> thrust of a merged union is the awesome meaning of what a
> national teachers union can do—call a nation-wide strike de-
> manding pay increases or other conditions that could paralyze

---

[20] New York *Times*, November 13, 1973.
[21] People Against Racism in Education, *Paper*, September–October
1973, p. 3.

the nation, and even wrest any remnants of control away from communities. This is the power union leaders, and teachers, and parents are much aware of. This is the kind of power which boards of education across the country would have to face at the negotiating table. What is a parent's answer to this threat?

It is critical for parents in New York City and other urban areas to consolidate their own strengths and to analyze strategies to outflank the Super Union. One strategy we suggest is that parents look carefully into each school to find and ally with those teachers who may be in the Union, but just don't buy into the unionism mentality. These are the teachers who work with kids at lunchtime and after school; who don't join the Union; who joined the Union only to be kicked around or out; who despair of the emptiness of their clock in-and-out existence. These teachers are scattered and all but invisible but they are there and they welcome collaboration with parents in the formation of real school communities.

Foremost, parents must recognize that *they do have power*. It is their children the teachers are hired to teach. If all else fails, they can and will set up their own schools. No children in public schools, no jobs.[22]

Teachers cannot close the doors of their classrooms to escape these forces. Parents and students are pushing from one direction, school administrators from another direction, politicians from yet another direction. Daily, teachers are being driven in a corner by greater demands in the classroom and diminishing public sympathy or respect. Their last resort is to protect themselves by unifying with a strong teachers' union. They become defensive—blaming parents for not doing their job well, the politician for not giving more money to the schools, etc.

During this game the personal lives of parents have also been affected. Parents are developing a new awareness that affects their psychic aspirations, and in this complicated

[22] Ibid.

society they feel that education is important to future success. Naturally, they want the best for their children. Only now some are not sure they are getting the best and others are quite sure they are not. Most families are unable to afford the prestigious private schools where many sense that quality education is still available. Parents become anxious when the reputation of a neighborhood school appears to deteriorate, when teachers strike, when new educational ideas are implemented without their knowledge.

But most of all they become anxious when their own child is having trouble. There is no more emotional connection between home and school than when problems arise with the child himself. Every parent knows the feeling associated with a school verdict that "your child is having difficulty." No parent wants his child to be unsuccessful. Consequently, any word that reports failure is psychically damaging for child and parent.

If a child comes home crying because of something that happened in school, the parent is being educated to view the school in certain ways. Further, if a child hates school and does not want to attend perhaps because of a certain teacher, then the seeds of conflict between home and school and teachers are planted at the most basic level.

What parent has not experienced his child not liking a particular teacher? Having a child live with a noncompatible teacher for a semester or year is damaging not only to child and teacher but to the parent as well.

Parents, like teachers, get together to compare notes. Images of particular teachers are formed at these sessions. Some teachers emerge with good ratings—others with quite negative ones.

Further, if parents try to do something about these individual cases, such as trying to transfer a child from one teacher to another, the school resists. The teachers affected might "lose professional face." Usually the principal must support his staff (otherwise he risks staff alienation).

The point is that the child is not served. His best interests are not always satisfied because of the way the school operates. The parents feel powerless. They must live with an unhappy child who is learning to hate school. The parent, wanting the best, fears his child's falling behind as a result. College and a good job—all are at stake. The parent becomes angry, seeks the support of other parents, and the seeds of collision are sown at still another level.

The seeds of collision between parents and teachers have been planted—economically, educationally, and psychologically. The soil is powerful, indeed. Parents and teachers were closer when they had the same agenda—what's best for the children. Because of the existing structure of the public schools and the growing politics in education there has been a shift. Through unionization teachers have had to give priority to their own welfare. Parents continue to display an ever stronger commitment to the child. These separate agenda items serve to disconnect the parties closest to the learner. Ultimately different priorities lead to conflict and collision. The results can hardly promote the growth needs of the learner—which is why schools exist in the first place.

II

COLLISION:
The Rise of Teacher Power

AT THE START OF EACH SCHOOL YEAR, we are almost at the point of asking, "Are the schools going to open?" "Are the teachers striking again?" As the 1972 school year was about to open, strikes were being threatened in countless school systems throughout the country. Teachers' organizations were busy in around-the-clock negotiations. A no-contract–no-work policy seemed to pervade the teachers and their professional organizations.

In America's largest city the threat of a teachers' strike elicited a concerned editorial from the New York *Times*, which stated in part:

> With the opening of the city's public schools only five days away, the United Federation of Teachers appears to have decided once again to move into the war of nerves routine in its contract negotiations with the Board of Education. Union president Albert Shanker's public display of pessimism is clearly intended to put pressure on the board to surrender to unreasonable demands in order to avert a strike.
>
> . . . At a time of extreme fiscal austerity and extraordinary need for instructional and administrative improvement of the

public schools, a settlement acceptable to the people of this city must give assurance that additional expenditures are inseparably linked to improved productivity.[1]

With the haunting memories of the ferocious 1967 and 1968 teachers' strike hanging over everyone, the threat of closing the nine hundred schools for the 1.1 million students seemed to enhance a last-minute settlement.

In Washington, D.C., 140,000 students and in Philadelphia 225,000 students were affected by strikes. By the end of September, at least ten districts in Pennsylvania remained shut by strike. Strikes continued in Racine, Muskego, and Appleton, Wisconsin. In Bridgeport, Connecticut, the strikers were pressing for settlement.

In Beacon, a small city in upstate New York, the strike seemed to come to be a test of strength for the new statewide teachers' organization, New York Congress of Teachers (NYCT).[2] A working teacher is quoted as saying, "This is a power struggle which goes far beyond our community." Another teacher is quoted as saying, "I think the BTA [Beacon Teachers' Association] is being taken advantage of. They're being used by their own leadership in Albany. NYCT is trying to make the Beacon Board of Education a scapegoat for the whole thing."

In Susquehanna Valley, New York, school closings prompted parents to keep the schools open by serving as teachers themselves. Many parents attended orientation sessions to assume their new tasks.

In Philadelphia, after a five-week impasse in the settlement of the longest school strike in that city's history, the arresting of two teachers' union leaders, the continued hiring

[1] New York *Times*, September 7, 1972.
[2] The name of the organization has since been changed to New York State United Teacher.

of substitute teachers, and the Board of Education's determination to keep the schools opened prompted labor leaders
to cry "strike breaking." The president of the city's AFL-CIO
Council (representing 300,000 union members) expressed
anger at the worsening situation—hinting that other unions
might have to join their union teacher colleagues on the
picket lines.

It is interesting to note that the mayors of both Philadelphia and New York had been elected with the help of
labor and the teachers. Ironically, in both prolonged strikes
(New York in 1968 and Philadelphia in 1973) labor began
to turn against both mayors, who were intimately involved
in unsuccessful negotiations.

In Philadelphia newspaper reports of the long strike revealed that the "public displayed little ire during the strike":

"After one noisy crowded meeting of the city council protesting crowds dwindled in the following weeks until there
were empty seats even in the reduced seating open to the
public."[3]

Teachers' strikes continued in the fall of 1973. Detroit, the
nation's fifth largest city, had the fall term begin with a
citywide teachers' strike, affecting 465,000 students and some
25,000 teachers. The Michigan Education Association and
the Michigan Federation of Teachers reported strikes in
Lansing, Jackson, Port Huron, and about twenty-three other
districts in the metropolitan Detroit area.

In Ohio teachers' strikes delayed the opening of schools
in Youngstown, Gallipolis, Athens, and other districts. Pennsylvania reported that at least eight school districts were on
strike.[4]

[3] *The Sunday Bulletin*, February 11, 1973.
[4] New York *Times*, September 5, 1973.

By the fall of 1973, inflation had further aggravated teacher negotiations. *Time* reported:

> Inflation has added to teacher agitation as spiraling living costs have negated salary increases. Beginning with a one-day walkout in August in Houston, teachers have struck in 86 communities across the country. In other cities, contracts were signed after marathon negotiations that ended just hours before classes began.[5]

Teachers' strikes continued into 1974 where the prolonged strikes in San Francisco and Kansas City were given national attention.

The rash of teachers' strikes revolves most notedly around money matters. Salary increases, cost of living raises, retirement benefits, and the like are steady items of negotiation. Only lately, school boards and city halls have been resisting proposed teacher salary packages for a couple of reasons.

The first reason is the tightening fiscal structure in state and local government. Most support of public schools is taken from property taxes. This dependence has reached a point in which the taxpayer is beginning to revolt. Until the problem of financing public education is resolved, a tight fiscal policy for education is likely to continue. This means that there will not be money to meet expanding educational demands, including teacher salary proposals.

Faced with such conditions, localities usually appeal to state legislatures for emergency funding. The entire procedure is obviously entrenched in politics so that uncertainties persist. During the past four years such major cities as Detroit, Chicago, Philadelphia, and Youngstown have not known whether they would have sufficient funds to complete the school year.

[5] *Time*, September 17, 1973, p. 59.

Consequently, when teacher negotiations reach an impasse these days, school and city officials will indicate that there simply is no money to give to teachers. Teachers will then strike, throwing the whole matter into a crisis status. Politically, few elected officials can take the position of raising taxes, especially when the citizens' pocketbooks are already overburdened—thus the stalemate continues.

Couple this morbid fiscal climate with the other pressing problem of declining educational quality in many urban schools and the situation gets even more complicated. Further, if teachers do strike, it is difficult for parents and other citizens to see how the quality of education can improve by keeping the schools closed. If anything, they see such moves as contributing to the deterioration. Many parents and students subjected to prolonged school strikes are placed in the precarious position of not knowing whether graduation will take place, whether college is possible. In brief, closing the schools means interrupted education for students, something few parents can tolerate. Those responsible must be reproached. The board of education, school superintendent, mayor, city council, are exhorted by the parents to "open the schools." When parents realize that the schools can only open by raising their taxes, many are faced by economics to review the situation anew.

In recent years the parents' anger turns back on the teachers and their bargaining unit. Other issues surface: Why should all teachers receive a salary increment? Why not only those who deserve it (those who are promoting learning with children)? Why not merit pay? But merit pay is opposed by teacher groups as discriminatory and divisive.

The public begins to realize that more money funded by the public schools does not mean more "production," i.e., more quality. What if teachers get more money? How do we know they will produce more?

Educational productivity therefore becomes a concern of boards of education as they begin to respond to parent pressure. The cycle of confrontation between public and professional, parent and teacher, continues as restrictive school financing, overburdening local taxpayers, traumatic interruption of family expectation occasioned by prolonged school closings, and concern for lack of educational productivity, and all conspire to fan the fires of collision.

The anger of parents and other taxpayers is also kindled when teachers' demands appear to mean more money for less work. In the 1973 strike in Chicago, the teachers' union demanded that the school year be shortened by two weeks, with no loss in teacher pay.

Another development that contributes to the growing rift between the public and the teachers' union is the current teacher surplus. This, coupled with declining student enrollments, produces a major fiscal strain for many communities. The report from a member of the San Diego City School Board is particularly revealing on this point:

> This fall we had a drop of 4,000 students and this necessitated terminating all 134 teachers we had hired last year, plus hundreds of paraprofessionals [teacher aides]. So the A.F.T. [American Federation of Teachers] jumped down our throats and we had to take back all but 34 of them. Now, you arouse the anger of the public when they read in the paper that our population dropped by 4,000 and yet we still have all those teachers on the payroll.[6]

Thus, at the start of the 1973–74 school year this public mood of uncertainty about what they were getting in return

[6] New York *Times*, September 12, 1973.

for their tax dollars in education became more evident. One reporter put it this way:

> Conversations with educators ranging from members of local boards of education to the top of the Federal education hierarchy disclose—beyond the physical shortages—a note of doubt about the direction of American public education as the new school year begins. The parents and public who pay for it, these officials said, seem unsure that they are getting their money's worth.[7]

The apparent locomotion toward collision between parents and teachers is now being identified at the grass-roots level. For example, in the summer of 1973, the Wisconsin Coalition for Educational Reform *Newsletter*, a volunteer grass-roots publication in Milwaukee, contained the following lead report entitled "Parents vs. Teachers????"

> . . . April 5th and 6th, the Wis. Congress of Parents and Teachers met and one distinct impression that came to me—no matter what the topic—was an alienation or hostility that has developed toward teachers. I have since checked my impressions with others who attended the convention and others who are in contact with parents, and they concurred with my estimation. As a parent concerned with the quality of schools, I am delighted to see this manifestation of unrest. It is unfortunate, however, to my way of thinking, that the anger seems to focus on just one element of the educational picture. I feel that all elements—School Boards, Administrative Personnel, and teachers—should be held up for equally critical scrutiny. I do hope that this feeling of discontent will spread into these areas so that they can be objectively viewed also. I hope, too, that parents soon feel the necessity to have their questions answered, their rights defined, and their roles in school matters expanded.
> In discussing the hostility I saw manifest toward teachers, the main area of concern was the teacher's militancy—not toward

[7] New York *Times*, September 12, 1973.

individual teachers, but toward the organizations, NEA, WEA, NTEA, and especially WEPAC. . . .[8]

Some parents are more direct concerning their solution to the problem of teacher power through strikes. For instance, during the teachers' strike of the Detroit public schools in September 1973, the Associated Press reported the following:

> . . . A check showed that some schools in Detroit were operating with supervisory personnel but there was little effort to hold regular classes.
>
> An exception was the Barton Elementary School, where parents groups helped out. "We will do whatever is necessary to keep the schools open," said Helen Moore, a spokesman for Black Parents for Quality Education. "If the teachers do not return, we believe they should be fired," Mrs. Moore said. "We don't want suburbanites on picket lines closing our black schools."[9]

This growing parental and public resentment of teacher power is slowly being noted by reporters. For instance, A. H. Raskin, veteran reporter and assistant editor of the editorial page of the New York *Times*, observed:

> . . . Strikes kept pupils out of classrooms for long stretches of the 1972–73 school years in the whole state of Hawaii, Chicago, Philadelphia, St. Louis and scores of smaller communities. But, in the new questioning mood toward public education, local school boards are finding that they are no longer weaponless in fighting back against union bulldozing. Far from caving in at the first wave of a picket sign, many communities welcome the attendant savings in teachers' salaries and other operating costs as a handy way to hold down overstrained budgets. Pay settle-

[8] Wisconsin Coalition for Educational Reform, *Newsletter*, Summer 1973, p. 1.
[9] New York *Times*, September 6, 1973.

ments have been moderate and capitulations to unions on educational policy rare.[10]

Now, when teachers strike, more parents find it difficult to understand how the children can profit educationally by not having school. In fact, many parents want to move toward a year-round school. They wonder why a summer vacation of one or two months is necessary. Many parents send their children to summer school or camp anyway (at extra expense to them).

Slowly parents are beginning to understand that the standard public school is still based on an agrarian economic cycle. At one time, the schools closed for the summer because young people were needed to work on the farm during harvest season. However, we are now an urbanized-suburbanized society with advancing technology, but the school structure has not kept pace with these developments nor with the expectations of parents and increased numbers of children.

A union position places teachers in a Marxism class-struggle situation. Teachers are exploited workers. The name of the game is to win back more dignity by demanding increasingly better wages and working conditions. Eventually, the teachers will become so organized that they will work against the "exploiters" (management)—which include boards of education, and school administration. They will liberate the teacher by making the teachers' union the controller. Having been oppressed, the teachers will rule with compassion.

In the meantime, unionized teachers are told not to commit themselves to "extra" work even if this work is for the purpose of trying to improve learning for children. Legislators responding to increased public reaction to higher costs of education begin to raise questions about heretofore untouch-

[10] December 17, 1973.

able areas such as teacher tenure. One Connecticut state-elected official is preparing a bill to end teacher tenure. If tenure is removed, then perhaps teachers can be held accountable for productivity.

David Sheldon, president of the American Federation of Teachers (AFT), is sensitive to the effects of the current "antiteacher" movement on the teachers themselves. He feels that teachers are fighting for their "psychic survival," explaining that teachers cannot experience failure day after day without serious personal consequence. Sheldon's point is crucial. The personal dimension is always basic. This current period of public accountability has begun to peel away the institutional layers, leading to the private world of the school and classroom. Teachers and other school officials are now exposed. Their private world is crumbling. They find it increasingly difficult to rationalize their problems. It was not too long ago when this private world provided them with easy access to psychic support. There was always the "teachers' room" where colleagues could meet over coffee to talk about "difficult classes" or the "impossible student." By comparing notes informally and by receiving peer reinforcement the teacher could get by.

Now with the avalanche of reviews on the "crises" in our schools, the public joins school people in knowing that teachers do not really know how children learn, what knowledge is most valuable, how best to teach, how best to organize a school, how to evaluate learning, etc. It is reasonable to assume that from certain quarters of this public will come the really harsh question: If you as professionals do not know the answer to these questions, then how do you know what you are doing? How can you continue to demand better wages when you do not know what you are doing?

While teachers' strikes and the struggle for power seem rather common practice these days, it was only about ten years ago when there were none at all. In 1961–62 the National Education Association (NEA), the largest professional teachers' organization, with 1.2 million members and 9,000 affiliated locals, reported exactly one strike. By 1970, it reported 181.

For some people, the visibility given the thirty-six-day 1968 New York City school strike brought the whole question of teacher power into the spotlight. The fierce nature of this strike between a teachers' union and the Ocean Hill–Brownsville Experimental School District of eight schools provided a glimpse of upcoming dangers and what appeared to be an inevitable collision between professional educators, led by teachers, and the public, led by parents.

Other people recall the statewide teachers' strike in Florida in 1968, which demonstrated the determination of both teachers and the public to hold the line, but with the public eventually winning out. The thirteen-week Newark strike in 1970 and the seven-week Philadelphia strike in 1973 provide further evidence of the battleground nature of public schools, especially those in our urban centers.

Few Americans perceive professional teachers' organizations as political instruments for obtaining increased teacher power. After all, teachers have been poorly paid, but they are dedicated. What teachers want is a decent wage. To be sure, this is why teachers did seek a strong union—to bargain for decent wages and working conditions. But the agenda seems to have gone beyond decent teacher wages, something most Americans would support. Robert Braun, education editor for the Newark *Herald Star Ledger*, began his book *Teachers and Power* by quoting a national organizer for the American Federation of Teachers:

". . . The American Federation of Teachers is determined to control the public schools of the United States. And someday it will. Just as the American Medical Association controls American medicine and as the American Bar Association controls the legal profession."[11]

For Braun, the teachers' union is engaged in a war for power and control:

Because it is a union first and foremost, its organization is geared to war, to servicing strikes, to collecting new members, to protecting teachers—whether or not they deserve protection —never considering the possibility that teachers, as surrogate parents, should really derive their true protection from the pure love they provide for their children and the respect they earn in a community, a neighborhood or a town. AFT leadership behaves like the leadership of any other established union—that is, with an eye to staying in power as long as possible. (A former union president is simply a teacher without a regular job, far away from the benefits of power and prestige.) Although it pays considerable lip service to local antonomy and union democracy, the national trains its reps to mold opinion, to exploit fears, if necessary, to promote paranoia and hysteria and even racism among its teachers, for the war must be won.[12]

But Braun also realizes that the public will not just take this power move lying down—or will it? "Public" is such an anonymous term. Probably most Americans still carry the image of a teacher as "the little old lady" dedicated almost completely to her work and removed from the pleasures and politics of real life. Teachers were once this way because the public viewed work with children in a protective way. That is, the public wanted to protect the children from the outside world. They screened teachers for their commitment to teaching and not to the outside world. Generally a woman was chosen and she was completely at the mercy of the com-

[11] Robert J. Braun, *Teachers and Power: The Story of the American Federation of Teachers* (New York: Simon and Schuster, 1972), p. 10.
[12] Ibid., p. 252.

munity. She had no private life and what she had was monitored. She was paid a notoriously low salary. In short, she was completely in the hands of an all-powerful school committee. It is now documented history that teachers were abused by the absolute power of the few who controlled the town.

Note the rules imposed on teachers at the turn of the century:

Teachers each day will fill lamps, clean chimneys and trim wicks.

Each teacher will bring a bucket of water and a scuttle of coal for the day session.

Make your pens carefully; you must whittle nubs to the individual tastes of the pupils.

Men teachers may take one evening each week for courting purposes or two evenings a week if they go to church regularly.

After 10 hours in school, teachers should spend their remaining time reading the Bible or other good books.

Women who marry or engage in unseemly conduct will be dismissed.

Each teacher should lay aside from each pay a goodly sum of his earnings for the benefit of his declining years, so that he will not be a burden on society.

Any teacher who smokes or uses liquor in any form, frequents pool halls or gets shaved in a barber shop will give good reason to suspect his worth, his intentions, integrity and honesty.

The teacher who performs his labors faithfully and without fault for five years will be given an increase of 25 cents per week in his pay if the Board of Education so approved.[13]

What was the teacher's reward for assuming such a saint-like role? Very little. And herein lies the tale. As the survival

[13] From a letter to the editor, Philadelphia *Inquirer*, October 24, 1972.

needs of teachers changed with the times, the old attitudes toward teachers persisted. Instead of rewarding the saintlike teachers with better wages and working conditions, those in control tried to keep the teachers politically weak by appeals to continue professional commitment and subsistence pay. This meant that teachers should not have an interest in salaries and other worldly things. But American economic and political forces did not keep pace with such noble values. Instead, the rewards went to those who were organized to receive them. Professional commitment of teachers was not rewarded—their show of unionized strength was. That is how our political-economic system works, and why teachers strike.

At first, boards of education called the bluff of AFT affiliates. When these affiliates proved that they could close the schools, the point where parents clamored for their reopening, the school boards began to take the threats of strikes seriously.

The UFT in New York, by far the most powerful AFT affiliate, contemplated a strike. It did so after considerable rank-and-file organization and after the significance of a strike was established with teachers. As the president of the UFT put it:

> . . . the teachers in many districts where strikes may occur are engaged in a soul-searching process. They, like countless groups of employees before them, are asking, "Is it really worth it? Can we, if we strike, possibly gain as much as we lose?" Those who answer negatively will be missing the point. In any strike, it is never possible to guarantee that, in the short run, the gains will make up for the losses. What is certain is that if teachers accept shabby treatment this time, they can expect the same treatment next time. If they stand fast now, it will alter not just this one set of negotiations, but all those which follow in the years to come—as well as their day-to-day relationships. . . .[14]

[14] "Where We Stand," New York *Times,* September 3, 1972.

Teachers' unions have learned this basic political lesson, as A. H. Raskin explains in the case of the United Federation of Teachers (UFT):

> In 1960, the U.F.T.'s less robust predecessor, the New York Teachers Guild, vainly sought to pry higher pay out of Mayor Robert F. Wagner, only to be told that the city had no money. Later in the school year the city was hit by a hurricane and by a heavy snowfall. In both cases, millions of dollars were quickly made available to clear the streets. When Shanker asked Wagner how come the city had money for these unbudgeted items, but none for teachers, the Mayor's answer was, "Al, those were disasters." Shanker now says: "That's when we decided to become a disaster."[15]

The image of the poor struggling schoolteacher is so much a part of our folklore that it is difficult to form a new image or to understand the reason for the rise in teacher militancy. Teachers have been historically oppressed, not only by the public but by the school itself. Inside the school, the teacher has been low person in a hierarchical chain.

Further, teachers have been dismissed for reading poems not on prescribed lists; for teaching about such topics as "civil disobedience"; for their political beliefs and the like—often without due process.

Indeed, the American teacher, once the political and economic doormat of our system of public education, is now part of a major movement to press for the exercise of increased teacher power. Over the past decade, teachers' organizations have mounted successful campaigns to mobilize and unify millions of teachers into potent political forces. The process for increased teacher power, in retrospect, now seems such a natural occurrence, given the oppressive conditions in which

[15] "Shanker's Great Leap," *New York Times Magazine*, September 9, 1973.

teachers found themselves earlier in this century. We have suggested that it was not too long ago when the teacher was the last to receive financial increases and the first to be replaced for any fiscal reason. Today the "schoolmarm" image is being replaced by that of a tough, disciplined urban teacher (equally divided between male and female), who is a member of a large professional organization. Today teachers have as much formal education as principals.

While this process of conversion seems natural to us now, the consequences have hardly surfaced and still evade most of us. Obviously, we sympathize with the American teacher as underdog. Who would question the right of teachers to decent wages and working conditions, or to freedom from any unfair lay and administrative oppression! The struggle for such rights triggered the formation of teachers' organizations in the first place. By uniting, teachers realized that they could better negotiate these rights. Yet, as rights were gained, teachers' organizations themselves increased their own status. They acquired a life of their own, almost apart from the classroom teacher. Teachers' organizations through negotiations became the spokesmen for masses of teachers. As with any organization, its own preservation and expansion assumed increasing priority. The irony that accompanies this inevitable cycle is frightening. Teachers, who hold the welfare of children in their hands, have delegated increased allegiance to their professional organizations, which, in turn, accept this increased responsibility and convert it into political power for escalating demands. By placing the organization ahead of all other considerations political power is established. More members join and seek the protection of all teachers (whether or not they deserve protecting). As this type of vested interest deepens, so does the negotiating authority of the organization, which, in turn, accelerates both the quantity and the quality of demands that favor teachers. While teachers' organizations fought for decent wages and working conditions, the public seemed sympathetic. But now teacher power has gone well beyond those "bread and butter" items. Now teachers' organizations are demanding a role in setting school policy in matters of finance and personnel. In short, teachers' organizations are seeking control of the schools themselves. Thus, teachers' organizations have fought for lower class size on the grounds that they would help children learn. Further, they have demanded the right of teachers to determine which children remain in school. Children considered "disruptive" would be placed in special classes or suspended from school.

While both these demands appear reasonable and would seem to provide a better classroom environment, the assumptions that undergird them are questionable. Reducing class size may make the classroom situation better for the teacher, but there is little evidence that reduction of class size alone improves learning. Further, expelling children who are labeled "disruptive" may also appear logical in improving the classroom climate. Yet many children labeled "disruptive" are simply not responding to the approaches being used with them. Classifying children as "disruptive" categorizes human beings in a manner that undermines the encouragement of growth and development—the central role of the school. Human classification may make conditions better for teachers, but it results in a system of self-fulfilling prophecies, in which those classified as "deviant" are isolated and not expected to perform and, indeed, do not perform as well as the "normals."

While teacher power grew during the sixties, other forces were also emerging which were destined to challenge the movement. One potent social development was the civil rights movement. The struggle for full service from the white-controlled institutions of America inevitably focused on the schools as the major instrumentality for gaining access to up-ward mobility, but the public schools were unprepared to respond. Desegregation of the schools was thought to provide blacks the same opportunities as whites.

The resistance to desegregation is now well-documented history. But black aspirations for quality education did not cease with resistance to desegregation. In advanced techno-logical white America, survival (economic and political) is dependent on good public education. Deprived of a chance for good education through desegregation, blacks sought greater control of their largely segregated neighborhood schools.

In the fall of 1966, the classic story of Intermediate School 201 in East Harlem unfolded. Intermediate School 201 sig-naled to many blacks an alternative path to quality education, an alternative steeped in American ideology—local control. I.S. 201 was to have been a model integrated school—this was the central school board's promise to the Harlem commu-nity. When I.S. 201 opened in the fall of 1966, the school was segregated. Vocal members of the community mobilized a strong protest in the form of a boycott, which made the front page of the New York *Times*. This event triggered the most serious reform for the New York City schools in decades —decentralization of schools, i.e., the subdividing of the mas-sive centralized school system into smaller districts, each with its own elected school board.

This move toward greater control of neighborhood schools also fit the changing complexion of the civil rights movement from dependence on whites for quality education (desegrega-tion) to black self-determination (community control).

Resistance to community control was almost more severe than that confronted by blacks with desegregation. The no-tion that blacks should control the budget, personnel selection, and curriculum smacked squarely into white racism and white control.

The organization that lead the resistance to decentralization and community control was the United Federation of Teachers. The 55,000-member affiliate of the AFT waged a fierce all-out campaign, including the expenditure of hundreds of thousands of dollars to defeat any strong state legislation that would have given serious authority to local communities. Not only was the UFT successful in thwarting real decentralization, they succeeded also in dismantling the demonstration districts which had been set up in the summer of 1967 as prototypes. Among the demonstration districts was the highly visible Ocean Hill–Brownsville, which became the subject of the thirty-six-day citywide teachers' strike. This prolonged shutdown of nine hundred public schools of New York brought the full political power of teachers' organizations into clear view. The UFT, realizing that it was fighting for its own future, unleashed its ultimate weapon—the citywide strike—denying over a million children schooling. Since schooling is one of the central values of modern society and essential for future success, denying New Yorkers access to formal schooling by closing most of the public schools became a potent social weapon. Ironically, the eight schools in the Ocean Hill–Brownsville demonstration district, whose action to transfer nineteen teachers triggered the strike, remained open. With this major action, the UFT brought the city of New York to its knees and frustrated the aspirations of many black and Puerto Rican communities seeking another chance for quality education. While the UFT won this particular battle, it had not actually won the war. (The use of military terms such as "battle" and "war" is most appropriate in describing the development in our schools. When any struggle for power and control is waged, adversary conditions are created.)

During the 1960s, the UFT in New York City areas had won important victories with the Board of Education in terms of wages, working conditions, hours of work, etc. Since teachers could (and did) bring the schools to a halt, they were a power group. Before teachers had unified, school administrators were the most potent group in the schools. The critical battles and wars by the teachers before the 1960s were against their intra-institutional enemies—the school administrators. Today school administrators cannot compete with the teachers' unions; i.e., they cannot bring the schools to a halt if they attempt a strike.

As teachers' organizations won the battles, they gained considerable prestige and confidence keeping the pressure on the Board of Education and the public for increased teacher power. As agents closest to the learner, teachers had a strong rationale for their demands. Moreover, as historical underdogs, the public identified with their attempts to gain a decent wage.

However, the exercise of power, as history teaches us, has a corruptive, self serving element. Teachers appear to be caught in this process.

But teachers are not the only power group; they are not the only ones who can bring the schools to a halt. Parents can do it—so can students themselves. These new power groups—teachers, parents, and students—surfaced during the 1960s as the key participants in the battlefield. In New York City, Intermediate School 201, Ocean Hill, and decentralization had given impetus to parents' power. As agents with an intrinsic concern for the positive growth of their children, parents had a legitimate role to play in setting school policy. Moreover, parents could serve as partial antidote to any group that would use the school for "clubhouse" politics. But parents do not have the time, the organization, or the finances to compete with established teachers' organizations. To be sure, parent organizations, such as the Parent Teacher Association and the United Parents Association, have attempted to keep parents involved, but in time of "war" a more expansive mobilization is necessary. The New York City parents learned that they could bring a school to an abrupt halt for a few days, perhaps for several weeks, but soon the pressure of other responsibilities would take over, gradually eroding their ranks. Children would return to school. All that the teachers' union had to do was to wait it out.

However, parents did learn some important lessons from this power game. They now realize that if their children are kept home, the schools cannot operate. Parent boycotts can be successful political devices—as we learned from the two-week East Harlem boycott in the late fall of 1972, involving Community School District 4. Protesting cuts in school services, the East Harlem Parents Council of District 4 led a strong boycott that closed thirteen of the eighteen schools in that community.

The Central Board of Education, responding to this political pressure, eventually responded to parent demands. The New York *Times* editorial assessed this event as follows:

> The East Harlem parents appear to have won their fight to restore some of the educational services which had fallen victim to local and Federal budget cuts. It is still unclear just how much money, and from what source, will be allocated to District 4 and to other hard-pressed districts throughout the city. But "new" money has apparently once again been "found."
>
> The scenario is particularly disconcerting because it is so familiar. Pleas of poverty by city agencies are followed by boycotts or other disruptive actions, and these in turn eventually pay off, quite literally, in cash that was not supposed to be there.

This procedure—by encouraging a continuous contest of escalating pressure tactics—is clearly destined to undermine orderly
government.[16]

The 1960s also witnessed the student movement.

Students, too, learned that they had considerable clout if
they organized for their rights. Students realized that they
could close the schools—without them, schools are meaning-
less. But students, like parents, suffered from lack of organization and money. Furthermore, it is hazardous for students
to confront adults who are able to hold strong sanction over
them, and teachers still control school marks and promotion.

Nonetheless, students did win several important battles.
Students rights policies were adopted in many school districts.
These policies included greater direct participation in pol-
icymaking. Student representatives were named on many
established councils and committees. Many high school Par-
ent-Teacher Associations became Parent-Teacher-Student Associations.

Obviously, as parent and student power increased, it challenged the aspirations of the teachers' organizations, which
were in high gear. The quest for power and control among
these parties of interest slowly turned former allies into enemies. Parents and teachers, long partners, now found themselves on opposite sides. This was especially true in minority
neighborhoods—black, Puerto Rican, chicano. Since AFT affiliates are more concentrated in urban centers where minorities live, the combats started with teachers' unions. For instance, in New York, Chicago, Newark, and Philadelphia,
where minorities make up the majority in public schools,
minority parents and students had skirmishes with teachers'
unions.

[16] December 7, 1972.

For many black and Puerto Rican parents and students, the teachers' unions now represents "the enemy." But it was not always this way. A few years ago, the AFT, itself an "underdog" within the bureaucracy, aligned itself with minority communities. The UFT seemed proud of its civil rights record. In fact, the late Dr. Martin Luther King himself praised the union efforts. The turning point from ally to enemy came during the initiation of the Intermediate School 201 demonstration district. The union leadership had spent months negotiating a proposal with an Intermediate School 201 negotiation committee comprising parents and residents. These sessions were held largely in private. The proposal for a pilot decentralized district of five schools (four elementary feeder schools and one intermediate school) with its own local board composed of parents, teachers, and community residents that would decide policy was not only new, but threatening to other school personnel including rank-and-file teachers who had not been involved in the months of discussions.

Further, the UFT had wanted the programs in the demonstration district to be modeled after their own MES (More Effective Schools), with its smaller classes and remedial help. MES was an important condition for the UFT. If such programs were tied to decentralization, then teachers would be more willing to support the plan. However, neither the New York City Board of Education nor the Ford Foundation, which had been an interested third party, agreed to support a MES program. The cost of MES seemed prohibitive considering the limited student gains reported. With the withdrawal of MES, the attitude of the union cooled. Further, as the experimental district began to unfold, the local governing board began to take seriously the matter of establishing personnel policies and made overtures concerning the screening of teachers. The UFT leadership, having lost on MES, could hardly stand by while a local group began to tinker with teacher security. This became apparent when rank-and-file teachers began to express alarm over the demonstration districts. Since most classroom teachers had little knowledge of the role that their union leaders had played in the initiation of the districts, when talk of screening teachers was heard, the rank and file turned their fears toward their leaders, who began to respond directly to these fears with a get-tough-on-the-pilot-districts policy. The leaders could have attempted to alleviate fears by explaining the long sessions with the community, the newness of the experiment, its importance given the crisis in American education—in short, by assuming a statesmanlike stance. As it turned out, they catered to the initial fears of the teachers, and this has made all the difference to the future directions of the UFT and the AFT.

But this is all hindsight. The fact remains that a small number of organizers are increasingly calling the shots for thousands of teachers. In so doing, they are gradually denying parents, students, individual teachers, and the public any real voice in the affairs of public schools. This small group of organizers has been referred to as "soldiers" by Robert Braun: "They are soldiers, and it is wartime in the public schools. . . ."[17]

During such times it makes political sense to unify teachers. In April 1972 a merger was announced by New York State between the 55,000-member UFT and the 105,000-member New York State Teachers Association. This merger was hailed as a historic feat, which it was. Aside from resolving their historical differences, the AFT and NEA affiliate agreed to form a New York State Congress of Teachers, subsequently changed to New York State Union of Teachers.

[17] *Teachers and Power*, p. 12.

This new organization united the teachers of New York against the common enemy—the lay public—a public grown weary of spiraling education costs and a scholastic deadline. Spokesman for this new mood of public fiscal sobriety was the state legislature, which responded to public discontent with get-tough policies on education. During the early 1970s, the legislature began to raise questions about professional tenure, one of the pillars of security for educators. In addition, a number of state legislature had entertained the possibility of considering performance contracting, i.e., allowing boards of education to contract with private enterprise for the delivery of instructional services.

Decentralization, community control, increased parent participation, performance contracting, flirting with such sacred values as tenure, public defeats of school taxes, all alert the leaders of teachers' organizations that the public mood toward schools will be hostile. How to combat these dangerous demands becomes the key issue needing organizational attention. Teachers, divided by two rival professional organizations, offer a weak defense. Two competing teachers' organizations debilitate the political muscle necessary to engage an angry public. The best strategy is to unite in the interests of teachers against their common adversary, which has now become the layman.

One of the key teachers' union leaders is reported making this antiteacher movement clear to his colleagues:

> . . . major attacks are being mounted on teacher pensions and on collective bargaining. This presents us with a situation that we have not previously faced.
>
> Up to now, teachers have had going for them the public's willingness to give money, if available, to schools. Now we are hearing arguments that, even if we have the money, we shouldn't give it to schools and certainly not to teachers.

These arguments appeal to two kinds of people—liberals and conservatives—and we must organize very carefully to bring our political weight to bear on behalf of education.

Noting that the new, merged state organization had done comparatively well in the state legislative interests, Shanker pointed out that teachers still faced a very crucial session of the legislature in which attempts to promote vouchers and performance contracting, limit collective bargaining, abolish tenure and revise pensions downward would certainly be made. . . .[18]

Schoolmen with long years of formal education were quick to seize a new banner of professionalism. They were the experts. Their expertise differentiated them from a lay public. As experts, it was they who knew what would be best for children—not the public, not even parents. They needed to stick together against these outside attackers.

Of course, they reasoned, as schoolmen, their professional status would not be used to alienate parents. Professional educators would keep the public informed by entering into a legitimate form of "public relations." Such public relations would serve to inform, to interpret to the public what the profession was doing.

Accountability—of course, there was to be accountability—would be professionally determined and supervised. After all, the doctors and lawyers police their own work ranks, why not educators? As persons of good will, professionals would discipline themselves so that mediocrity would be controlled.

A professional was someone who knew more than a layman and, therefore, should make the basic decisions affecting children. This philosophy increasingly permeated preparatory programs in education intended to bring the skills of educators in line with those of other professionals. There was no deliberate thought of denying the public any of its rights or of

[18] *New York Teacher*, Vol. 14, No. 14 (December 3, 1972), p. 5.

seeking to control the school system itself. This came later as professional organizations entered the political arena. Public accountability and antiteacher sentiment provided a new climate for considering the unification of the nation's teachers.

According to the president of the United Federation of Teachers, the national movement toward teacher unionism constitutes a "Quiet Revolution."

Over the past decade America's three million public school teachers have staged a quiet but prodigious revolution. They have done what other workers did 40 years ago; they have organized.

The revolution began as a movement with limited objectives. Teachers sought to improve their salaries and working conditions. They wanted benefits and protections that other workers had already won.

To achieve their goals, teachers adopted the tactics and strategies that these other workers had created.

Prior to 1962, not one collective bargaining agreement existed in any of the nation's 10,000 school districts. Today negotiated contracts cover nearly 60 percent of all teachers.

Nowhere in 1962 did teachers enjoy a legal right or organize and bargain collectively. Today those rights are recognized in the laws of 27 states; and teachers bargain in several other states where there are no laws.

Before 1962 teachers had rarely conducted strikes. Neither of the national teacher organizations—the AFL-CIO American Federation of teachers and the unaffiliated National Education Association—favored strikes, considering them "unprofessional." Today teacher strikes are common; and both national groups endorse strikes as a "last resort" weapon.

Prior to the 1960's teacher organizations rarely participated in partisan politics. They prided themselves on staying out of election campaigns, and actually believed they could keep education and politics separate. Today teachers are a major political force in several states; and their organizations recognize that every gain and every loss, and every goal and every danger is achieved ultimately—is produced or protected—through the political process. There simply is no separating education and politics.

And in 1962 barely 50,000 teachers belonged to unions affiliated with organized labor; most teachers considered fraternizing with working-people—the parents of their own pupils, and the ultimate consumers of their product—undignified and unprofessional. Today nearly 400,000 teachers enjoy affiliation with the AFL-CIO, and their numbers are rapidly increasing.

Each of the elements of this revolution has been important to the successes teachers have achieved. Nationwide their salaries have jumped more than 100 percent. They enjoy extensive fringe benefits, including some of the country's best pension systems.[19]

The UFT president also sees the other labor union oriented workers as the best allies of teachers—this includes affiliation with the AFL-CIO.

But of all the elements in their revolution, teachers have given less credence to AFL-CIO affiliation than to any other. That is now changing. Teachers have come to the same conclusion which other workers reached long ago. Every group of workers is an integral part of our society; no group can go it alone; and each of us needs allies.

Other workers are teachers' natural allies because they share patterns of organization, tactics, strategies and goals. If teachers want higher salaries and better pensions, so do factory workers, airline pilots, and the musicians of the New York Philharmonic. The taxes of these workers help pay teachers' salaries, and help make educational improvements possible. Over the past decade teachers have won as much as they can on their own; they cannot make further gains without the active support of the American workers. And they can win that support only if they extend their own support to others, so that other workers can enjoy benefits equal to those that teachers have won.

[19] "Where We Stand," New York *Times*, October 29, 1973.

Nor can teachers single-handedly fight off the many attacks now made on their profession, and even on the public schools as an institution. The critics of teachers and schools—supported by a peculiar alliance of liberal academics, giant foundations, profit-minded businessmen, and conservative public officials—propose an endless array of cure-all gimmicks that would, at the very least, strip teachers of their new- and hard-won gains, and, at the extreme, dismantle the public schools altogether. Only the working-class, to whom the promise of education has always been the most real and meaningful, joins teachers in the defense of the public schools. And no institution in American life has a longer and deeper commitment to the public education than has the organization of that working-class, the AFL-CIO.[20]

It is clear to the UFT head who the allies of teachers are *not:*

Teachers will not find allies in the news media. When they were struggling and powerless they did, as farmworkers do today; but any union faces criticism in the media once it is organized and successful. *Nor are parents, as parents, the allies of teachers; in any strike parents think more of their own inconvenience than of the merits of the teachers' cause.* Chambers of commerce, blocs of manufacturers and leagues of businessmen are at best disinterested in raising their own taxes to pay teachers better, or even to finance direct school improvements.[21]

Since it is clear that teachers' unions can no longer count parents as their allies, then they (parents) must be classified increasingly as "the enemy." It is clear from such statements not only that teachers need to pursue their own agenda but that they must "take on" parents, if necessary. As laymen who would hold teachers accountable in unfair ways, and who place their own interests and those of their children ahead of those of teachers, parents cannot be counted on

[20] Ibid.
[21] Ibid.

during this "wartime" period. Certainly, the seeds of political collision are planted by such calls to action. Further, if the disconnection of parents and teachers is accentuated by unionization, then the existing process of child growth and development is placed in jeopardy. As we have emphasized before, parents and teachers are two of the basic agents in the learning process of the young. When they are co-operating, the factors that provide learning can be more ably orchestrated. When these two socializing agents are at war—the consequences on child development—the central function of the schools will be irrevocably harmed.

To be sure, politicians are now quite sensitive to community sentiments about schools—their jobs could depend on it. As the public mood began to change toward teachers, so did that of the legislature. Sensing all of these developments, the union leadership forged ahead with attempts at merging the two giant organizations—NEA and AFT.

The National Education Association, the largest of the two teachers' organizations, has gone through a number of stages which increased its militancy. Labeled a company union until the 1960s, the NEA has received mounting competition from the American Federation of Teachers, which had joined the union movement in this country. More important, the AFT adopted a strong political strategy for improving teacher salaries and working conditions. By forming a scrappy teacher-oriented union, the AFT was able to lobby effectively in Washington and in state capitals. Until recently the NEA retained its loose structure, which included all professional educators and administrators, as well as teachers.

As the pressure from the public grew, teachers sought more protection from the NEA, but the structure made quick action difficult. The Classroom Teachers, the largest subunit of the NEA, threatened to form a new and separate organization. Classroom teachers were looking for a tough-minded leadership and an alert organization to deal with contemporary concerns. Basic changes have taken place within the NEA headquarters in Washington, D.C. Several administrative groups have withdrawn from the NEA and moved to new quarters because of the internal splits now occurring. There are many professional educators who view with alarm the move of the NEA toward a teachers' union. Today the NEA is composed primarily of classroom teachers.

Throughout the country, many NEA teachers looked with awe at the achievements of the AFT teachers, and talk of a merger grew. The old NEA structure made the elected president of the NEA a figurehead who served for only one year. The real authority of the NEA has historically been with the hired staff, led by an Executive Secretary. However, as teacher militancy grew, so did demands for strong leadership.

In the late 1960s a shift in power between the president of the NEA and the executive secretary began to be in evidence. In the 1972 convention, calls for reform in the structure took on priority. Watching on the sidelines was a confident AFT and UFT. Shortly before a vote on a change in NEA organization, the president of the UFT devoted an entire advertisement column on the NEA issue. The column indicated:

. . . Structurally, the NEA resembles a government of latter-day Manchu. In the provinces are a series of warlords: the hierarchies of the 50 state associations. Each state group is a separate corporation. Most are dominated by an appointed and self-perpetuating staff in collusion with school administrators. The staff is far less interested in building a strong teacher organization than in holding power within NEA and in wielding power to exact tribute—in money, NEA staff assistance, and a range of personal favors and prerogatives.

. . . Those progressives who recognized its structure as the cause of NEA's ineffectiveness despaired of piecemeal reform. They called for a Constitutional Convention to overhaul the entire system. "Con-Con," as it came to be known, was launched in 1969. For two years its planners sought the views of every NEA member, of all affiliated groups, of outside experts—of anyone who had any opinion at all. Con-Con's 500 elected delegates met for three weeks in the summer of 1971. They produced drafts of a new Constitution and Bylaws. Reaction was solicited from every quarter. The delegates reconvened in the spring of 1972 and revised their drafts. And when it is all over, Con-Con will have cost the NEA nearly $1.5 million.

. . . In sum, the Con-Con documents would make NEA an effective organization. They democratize the Association by transferring power from the staff to elected leaders. They create a single, 30-member Board elected at the national Convention; its members would reflect national concerns and would run on nationally-oriented platforms. The proposed Constitution and Bylaws also lengthen the terms of officers to two years and permit re-election two times. And they reduce the influence of state hierarchies and other pressure groups by basing NEA governance on the local association—the unit closest to the NEA member.

. . . NEA members have a better option. They can vote "yes" on Con-Con, and help create an Association capable of doing the job they want it to do.[22]

In assessing the experience of the past decade and its significance to the educational profession, especially the NEA, the president of the United Federation of Teachers comments:

. . . It has not been an easy decade. The first task was to convince the teachers themselves—against the opposition of the National Education Association (NEA) and its affiliates, who then

[22] "Where We Stand," New York *Times*, October 15, 1972.

shunned collective bargaining, militancy and strikes as "unprofessional labor tacts"—that collective bargaining was a good thing. As a result of union victories during these years, the NEA and most of its affiliates have abandoned their old views and adapted union approaches and methods.[23]

Clearly, the paths were being cleared for national merger. The teachers of America were all experiencing public pressures and were in need of bold leadership, which would protect their interests.

The NEA, founded by Horace Mann, has been dedicated to noble principles of professional education. Since 1857 when it was organized, the NEA has maintained this purpose: "To elevate the character and advance the interests of the profession of teaching and to promote the cause of popular education in the United States." While the NEA won recognition as reflecting the ideals of the profession, political battles were being waged in the schools. Improving professional status in the political arena required lobbying, rank-and-file organizations, disciplined responses—in short, unionized forms of organization.

Merger talks proceeded between the AFT and NEA in 1973–74. Support for a merger is being led by NEA educators from urban centers, where the problems are more concentrated and the public pressure more pronounced. This trend of the NEA toward increased militancy follows that of the AFT, itself largely an urban-dominated union. While the problems of public education are first manifested in city schools, they are spreading as urbanization itself spreads nationally. Teachers in big city schools are the first to be subjected to both the internal and the external politics of con-

[23] Ibid., October 31, 1971.

temporary public education. They need the protection of a strong professional organization.

In most big cities teachers have begun to switch from the NEA to AFT affiliation. In some cities membership is divided between each major professional association.

The tough-line stance of the AFT becomes increasingly attractive to teachers sensing the growing public harassment. The NEA has historically represented the professional ideals of the educators (including commitment, public responsibilities, playing down the so-called bread and butter items: better pay and working conditions and teacher security). The latter have been the priority items for the AFT. They have gained potency within the teaching ranks for having a good track record in this area.

To achieve their "bread and butter gains," the AFT has had to become politically astute. The NEA until recently had tried to keep out of "politics."

Some argue that the merger might achieve a blend balancing the professional with political concerns. Others feel that the NEA would be surrendering its professional reputation to a union that considers professionalism as of secondary importance. Consequently, the early attitude of the NEA was positive toward merging with the AFT but not with AFL-CIO. However, it is precisely this link with organized labor that gives the AFT so much latent clout.

Consequently, if teachers are unified nationally, preferably as an AFL-CIO affiliate, they would be prepared for the political battleground that is forming. Obviously, with a hard-nosed union orientation the leadership would be ready to engage the enemies of the schools.

For those who would raise questions about any possible professional compromise by being unionized, there is always the reminder that if things get rough there is nothing like receiving help from other union locals. Together organized labor can cripple a city, state, or nation.

The prolonged and bitter teachers' strike in Philadelphia during the winter of 1973 was settled in part by the threat of forty local unions to join the teachers in a citywide strike.

There is an underlying sentiment that if merger were consummated the AFT leadership would become the heir apparent of a giant national union of teachers. However, at present an internal battle is being fought for leadership of the AFT. The odds are that the president of the UFT will emerge as the ultimate leader because of his strong identification with the AFL-CIO. Ironically, it is this affiliation with labor that has resulted in NEA resistance to merger.

Naturally, it is difficult to put aside the basic differences that characterize the AFT and NEA. And the differences have indeed been basic. After all, it was only a few years ago during the heat of the school decentralization issue in New York City that the NEA passed a resolution favoring decentralization of large urban schools. This in direct opposition to the stance taken by the AFT on decentralization. The AFT is, first of all, a union. As such, it is aligned with AFL-CIO labor in the United States. This has two sides to it. Of course, if unionized teachers get into serious trouble, they have the weight and resources of organized labor to back them up. In practical terms, should teachers strike and the going get rough, other unions could muster walkouts until a town, city, state, or nation became critically affected. There is no doubt that labor could bring the entire country to a halt if the stakes were high enough.

While this alliance with labor has provided muscle, there are also negatives. Unionized teachers pay a price for this support. Every teacher, in favor or not, must be prepared to give the same support to other unions. This could affect the operation of schools.

Further, as a teachers' union, the tactics utilized are likely to be labor-oriented. The commitment aspects of being a professional, some argue, are lost under a union organization. Also, because of the management-labor dichotomy, the public school is split into sides, with the object of the game being to negotiate a contract on every aspect of school operation. Precise legal wording is used to pinpoint length of school days for teachers, what duties they should or should not perform. Work stoppages and strikes are the weapons used in case an acceptable contract for package is not negotiated.

Leading this move toward merger is Local 2 of New York City. New York City seems to face most problems before other cities. New York City had the first race riots in the summer of 1964. It was the first city to deal with the problem of school decentralization. In the several strikes undertaken by the UFT, the most bitter and critical was the thirty-six-day affair with Ocean Hill.

Capsulated into the episode were all the forces that viewed the public schools as a major battlefield. As such, it could be a sneak preview of coming attractions for the nation. New York City seems to be at one extreme point on a continuum to which all other quarters of the nation are also connected at some point. The UFT, representing the professional educator (the supervisors' association had thrown in with the teachers), was on one side of the battlefield, and the Ocean Hill representatives, the lay public, on the other. The fact that Ocean Hill was a black community added more fuel to the political fire, but the lines of public-professional were clearly drawn here. The Ocean Hill governing board had attempted to transfer nineteen teachers. This was the board's way of testing who controlled the schools. The UFT retaliated immediately, closing all of the schools but those in Ocean Hill (one of the three demonstration districts). Every citizen of New York was made aware of the crisis. Few citizens understood the issues underlying the battle. What most people knew was that the schools were closed. Kids were on the streets. Parents, whose household schedule depended on their children attending school, grew angry, became outraged, and placed pressures on elected officials—most notably, the mayor.

The UFT kept the pressure on and aggravated it with talks of black anti-Semitism, which flared further the emotions of the public. The ferocity of the battle grew, expanding the political participants to include state officials, civil rights groups, etc.

The point here is that the UFT, fighting one of the major battles of the war, successfully used its ultimate weapon. In the process, it also learned that schooling was necessary for consumers, regardless of its quality. They will do almost anything to keep it going. If schooling were denied the public, this could become a potent political lever to be used at appropriate times.

By waging such battles, the UFT and its leadership have gained a national reputation. Not all of this image is positive, however. In certain quarters of the teaching profession, the strategies and tactics utilized are viewed with caution. Many fear an ultimate take-over by the New York City local.

But the UFT, AFT, and NEA have won battles that improve their power with the existing system, not a reformed one. Together, they are now the most powerful group controlling a public school system that is centralized, monolithic, and uniform. They are winning, and their prize is the standard system. Teachers' organizations now prefer a centralized structure. It's easier to maintain control of the schools this way. Decentralizing the public schools runs counter to this trend, so it must be challenged.

When teachers' unions were low men on the totem pole, they criticized the system, but, naturally, when they become "top dog," the system looked far better to them. Ironically, teachers' unions are now placed in a situation in which they must defend the system as adequate, needing only extra money to improve. Since they wield much of the power within the public schools, they find it increasingly easy to dismiss any reform proposal that fundamentally alters the status quo. The UFT has publicly opposed most serious plans to reform the New York City schools, including the decentralization proposals and those of the Fleischmann Commission.[24] Their platform for reform remains MES—a compensatory approach which adds more personnel and resources to the existing structure.

That the leadership of the UFT is compelled to fight for the status quo is also observed by ranking New York *Times* reporter A. H. Raskin:

> But pragmatist Shanker assigns such high priority to protecting all those with a vested stake in the existing school structure, particularly his teachers, that his derogators dismiss his protestations of interest in educational change as lip service. . . .[25]

We repeat the scenario: rank-and-file teachers, afraid of the external forces that are converging on them, turn increasingly to their professional organizations for protection. In return for this protection, the teachers give up their individuality and their authority. This is delegated to a small

[24] A special governor-appointed commission to study the quality, cost, and financing of schooling in New York State.
[25] *New York Times Magazine*, September 9, 1973, p. 81.

group who will wage the protective war. All the rank and file need do is to co-operate, to follow faithfully the suggestions of the central leadership group.

With the UFT leadership having won ribbons for their feats in the New York City campaign, it was natural for them to provide direction to the state organization, the New York State Union of Teachers. As teachers around the state became subject to increased pressure from the public, the new state organization promised to protect them. This was like music to the ears of many teachers, and they gladly relinquished their limited authority in favor of a unified body. Now with over 200,000 organized teachers, the UFT could parlay its strategies and tactics to the state level. This time, Ocean Hill may be any school district in New York State. Let us hypothesize that in some school district teachers with several years' experience have been replaced by beginning teachers in order to save money. With the teacher shortage over, and with a surplus of unemployed teachers job hunting (school administrators report over three hundred teachers applying for each vacancy), replacing teachers is no big problem. Moreover, some report unemployed teachers willing to work for less money than appears on the suggested salary schedule for the district. These unemployed teachers are desperate. Many have families and need work. School systems, feeling the fiscal pressure, are tempted to hire teachers at beginning or lower salaries in order to save money.

However, if the state teachers' union permits this to happen, other school districts would follow. Clearly, the teachers are being threatened. This is, indeed, another Ocean Hill, and the public needs to be taught another object lesson. They can't tinker with teacher security. The state teachers' organization warns the school board to replace the experienced teachers or face the sanctions of the organization.

The school board may decide to call the bluff of the state teachers' union. This is followed by a statewide walkout of teachers—closing most of the public schools in the state. If this were to happen, many parents would rise up in rage: "What is going on here? Why should our schools be closed because District C is having problems? We want our schools open! Let District C solve its own problems—it's unfair!"

But this is precisely the intent of the strategy—to arouse public concern, to put pressures on District C to resolve the issue so that other schools in the state can return to normal.

Finally, enough pressure builds on political figures to get some action. If the events of Ocean Hill are repeated, then the state teachers' organization will emerge as a strong power group.

However, the forces that are at work are more complicated than that. Perhaps District C can counter the state teachers' union's threat of reprisal by threatening itself to fire any teacher who does not report for work, indicating that it has hundreds of applications from the surplus ranks of unemployed teachers. In short, should the employed teachers walk out, they can all be replaced by new teachers.

Let us suppose the state teachers' union decides to escalate the crisis by calling for a statewide strike by the members. The local board of District C attempts to hire new teachers, but there are pickets surrounding each school; those trying to get through the pickets are subjected to harassment. Police are brought in. Let us assume further that, with police protection, new teachers are able to assume their classroom assignments. The other schools of the state are still closed, but reports indicate that many teachers, figuring that their school board might do the same thing as District C, return to work.

Leadership attempts to get the teachers back on the picket lines may produce some change, especially if the argument is used that unless they do "stick it out," school boards will have the right to replace them.

If the situation is getting critical, the state teachers' union, because of its affiliation with labor, may plead for the union to help them. This may elicit some strike threats from other labor unions. Ultimately, if union interests are best served, other unions may walk off their jobs, crippling public services, thus escalating the battle.

All these activities will play havoc with the political scene. Unless politicians can resolve the issue, citizens will replace them. If the state teachers' organization wins the battle, then they would be assured even more power.

This would stimulate organizing at the national level. The battleground could now become the nation. If a school system threatened the interests of teachers, they would have to contend with not only a state but a national teachers' organization. What would happen if the public schools of the entire nation were closed? Think of the political pressures that would result!

The AFT leadership realizes that the stakes are indeed high. If the public call for accountability gets out of hand, the leaders' future is in serious doubt. However, if they could mobilize the teachers of the nation in time, the union could emerge as one of the most powerful political units in the country.

All of this is conjecture, of course, but how far from this stage are we? The prolonged Philadelphia teachers' strike was settled on the eve of a general strike by more than forty local unions supporting the teachers. The New York State merger has already been consummated. We have a New York State United Teachers. Discussions with the NEA have gone on over the past several years. By 1968, George Fisher, then the new president of NEA, assumed a more sympathetic

stance toward the merger. The Classroom Teachers of the
NEA not only had formed their own separate organization
but also appeared to be moving the NEA in a similar direction
as the AFT. Classroom Teachers are sensing the extensive
pressures on them and want strong protection from their professional organization.

The AFT has strong appeal to the frontline teachers. The
chances for achieving some form of merger in the long run
are good. As suggested, basic changes are now apparent in the
NEA headquarters in Washington, D.C. The union flavor has
already resulted in several NEA units moving to new quarters.
(Such organizations as National Elementary Principals Association, National Secondary Principals Association, American Association of School Administrators have broken away
from the NEA.) Should merger occur, many believe that the
AFT would infiltrate the merged organization and gradually
take over. It is the most prepared for "warfare."

The forces that are occasioning this collision continue to
press all parties of interest against the monolithic public
school structure. It is this institutional structure that is the
biggest problem in the avoidance of the collision. Further, this
system is molding the attitudes and behaviors of those inside
it, for existing institutional arrangements in part shape the
people within them. Teachers' unions come to accept the
existing system as legitimate—negotiate to protect it—and so
the battlefield conditions persist.

The point has to be made repeatedly that teachers have
been driven to organize and respond in this way. An unresponsive hierarchy in which each layer did its respective job
created many unfair conditions for the teacher. Poor pay, no
due process protection (so that arbitrary dismissals were
common), overloaded schedules, unreasonable control over

the private life of the teacher, etc., forced teachers to stick together in order to improve their lot, and this sticking together has produced significant improvement for teachers. The 1972 New York City schools' three-year teacher contract called for a $20,350 maximum for classroom teachers, security and tenure improvement, and a host of other benefits. Clearly, without such a strong union, teachers would hardly have been able to show such results.

This entire movement was made possible by an uninformed public. The public wanted teachers to be professional, but expect them to be satisfied with abnormally low salaries and benefits. The public did not reward teachers before they organized. Instead, the elected officials rewarded those teachers who could organize into powerful political blocs. Once this began to happen, the public then criticized the teachers for losing their professionalism.

Heads of teachers' organizations are not subjected to public accountability, as are school boards or schools administrators. Yet leaders of teachers' unions wield considerable influence with the educational system. This immunity from public control gives the head of the teachers' association a special advantage. He can engage in all kinds of activities, be as close to school events as any school administrator, yet be free from civilian review.

Further, school administrators need the protection and muscle a strong teachers' union can provide. Such "co-operation" and/or dependence places the supervisor in an awkward position when it comes time to evaluate teachers, to determine which ones should receive tenure, etc.

Now, an uninformed, unresponsive public must pay the price for forcing teachers into these strong political organizations. While teachers' organizations focused on such basic items as salary, working conditions, due process, and the like, the public, including boards of education and their administrative staff, did seem to understand and accept this form of negotiation.

Therefore, once the journey into the domain of organized power reaches a certain stage, it has a natural tendency to expand. That is to say, teachers' organizations have moved their negotiations from the commonly accepted bread and butter item, such as salary, into the realm of educational policy—heretofore the domain of a lay board of education. Once teachers' organizations deal with matters of policy— in such areas as *personnel* (including hiring and firing), *budget* (including where limited funds are allocated), *school organization* (how a school is organized for learning), *student personnel* (how students are grouped, which student remains in school, etc.)—once these public responsibilities are relinquished, then an almost absolute *professional monopoly* will have been achieved. As teachers' organizations seek to emulate the power and control of the other professions— most notably, the medical and legal professions—they will move toward a national merger of classroom teachers. With such an organization, they could, indeed, bring the entire system of American education to an abrupt halt. Such awesome potency, at the very time when the American public is placing higher priority on education, will place enormous pressure on the public for quick settlements. This means teacher demands will continue to increase and the public will continue to meet them, or else (or else face the condition that children will not receive an education).

At first, the public will give up a lot in order to keep the schools open. Many will even identify with the demands of teachers. But ultimately, they will realize that they have given up their own rights in the process.

The teachers' union's first negotiated contract under New York City school decentralization, with its thirty-one community boards in 1972, began to reveal the public's attitude toward professional infringement in policy areas. The New York Lawyers' Committee for Civil Rights Under the Law, in its Community School System newsletter, reviewed the contract, indicating:

Six months ago, the negotiating process for the new teacher's contract began. From the beginning it was clear that salary would not be the crucial issue. The general expectation that the union would settle for a wage package within the federal 5.5% guidelines proved to be correct. The hard-fought negotiating really took place on the non-monetary matters.

Community board negotiating council representatives took a hard line against union demands which they felt went beyond valid concern with working conditions and encroached on the board's policy-making prerogatives or rights under decentralization.

The union's 700-item list had included such "policy" demands as a right to prevent any lay-offs in response to budget cuts, elimination of the bilingual license and control over conditions for appointment of supervisors, among others. At a time when the city-wide aspects of the school system have been limited by decentralization, the union also sought to extend and strengthen inter-district policies governing transfers and excessing and to establish various other new city-wide rules.

In response, many community board members called not only for resistance to the new demands, but also for a roll back of existing contractual provisions which have limited community board discretion on appointments, transfers, dismissals and educational experiment. The community board's position was supported by legal research. Precedents cited in a memorandum prepared by the Community School System Project indicated that many of the new demands, and many items in the old contract, including the well established class size limitation, were indeed matters of "policy" beyond the lawful scope of the bargaining on "working conditions" sanctioned by the Taylor Law. . . .[26]

Further, teachers' unions will gain considerable expertise in public relations. They will always attempt to create an image of teachers as the oppressed, making very balanced demands—such as smaller classes. They will attribute positive qualities to their "enemies" after each teacher contract, e.g., "We could not have done this without the support of the parents and other citizens."

In New York City the United Federation of Teachers is able to maintain a weekly column in the Sunday New York *Times* called "Where We Stand." This column is actually a paid UFT advertisement located prominently on the widely read education pages of "The Week in Review" section. With such a platform, the UFT can "take after" anything and anyone—without real worry that "equal time" will be offered to any of the "victims" in these columns. It is highly unlikely that other groups like parents or students have the organization, muscle, or finances to command the same attention in one of America's most prestigious newspapers.

That the UFT uses this weekly column for its own propaganda purposes is surely obvious and to be expected. The reaction to this column by those who have been subjected to attack is also to be expected.

Writing in the *Harvard Education Review*, Allen Graubard, an advocate of alternative education and author of *Free the Children*, responds to one column on public school alternatives:

". . . Alternatives inside the public sector supported by local, state or federal aid are sure to spread in the near future.

[26] "The New Teacher's Contract—An Overview," *Community School System Law Letter*, Vol. 1, Issue 4, p. 2.

A recent column by Albert Shanker in the weekly propaganda slot the teachers' union buys in the New York Sunday *Times* confirmed this assertion. Shanker attacks the claims of success for alternative schools—in a misleading and dishonest manner. But his tone is very defensive, as if against a growing trend he opposes. . . ."[27]

In one prominent case, Professor Marilyn Gittell, noted political scientist at Brooklyn College, was subjected to a harsh attack for her role as a participant in the formulation of several major studies of the New York City school system, including the Bundy Decentralization Report (strongly opposed by the UFT in 1967–68). The column warned foundations not to provide support for Dr. Gittell because her major goal is to engender conflict.

In a reply published in the New York *Times* the following Sunday, January 28, 1973, Dr. Gittell responded:

> It is clear that Mr. Shanker's attack on my personal and professional integrity last week in his regular advertisement was not to present an honest appraisal of the issues. It was a blatant character assassination intended to quiet an academician who has tried to make the facts available to a larger public, and because those facts challenge the union's position, Mr. Shanker has little regard for academic freedom and independence when the facts directly contradict what he would like us to believe. In tying his character assassination of me to certain foundations involved in educational research, Mr. Shanker has informed all foundations that he will also attack them when independent studies carried out under their auspices do not agree with his views. There is another motivation in Mr. Shanker's attack on me. He hopes thereby to undermine parent slates and community participation in community school board elections in March. In that way the union's bank roll will be the only source of financing for the "right kind" of slate.

[27] *Harvard Educational Review*, Vol. 42, No. 3, August 1972, p. 372.

The president of the UFT continued to press his opposition to Dr. Gittell on the occasion of her being considered for appointment as associate provost and assistant vice president of Brooklyn College. The New York *Times* reported:

Mr. Shanker's attack on Dr. Gittell's qualifications as a scholar and what he assailed before the Board of Higher Education as her "anti-union ways" has kept a controversy simmering in the City University community over what several Board officials considered Mr. Shanker's attempt to limit Dr. Gittell's academic freedom.

Conversations with the main characters in the incident, however, suggest that the argument between Mr. Shanker and officials of the Board go beyond the issue of academic freedom alone.

The dispute began in late November when Mr. Shanker appeared in person before the Board of Higher Education which was then considering Dr. Gittell's transfer from Queens College to her new post at Brooklyn College. According to a board transcript, he asserted that Dr. Gittell's appointment would "threaten the entire relation that exists between our union and the City University."

Mr. Shanker called the proposed appointment "the equivalent of the appointment of George Wallace as head of the Brooklyn College Education Department," and said Dr. Gittell had, for the last six years, "devoted her entire career to destroying our union."

"We have no alternative than to see this in terms of our relation with the City University," Mr. Shanker concluded. Some board officials took his remarks as a threat to limit cooperation by his union with various City University programs involving student teachers in the public schools.

"It was the first time I really felt myself eyeball to eyeball with a threat to academic freedom," said one high-ranking member of Chancellor Robert J. Kibbee's administration, who asked that his name not be used.

Other officials called Mr. Shanker's short statement "a direct personal attack" on Dr. Gittell and lamented the unprece-

dented permission he had been granted to address the closed
meeting on a personal matter.

"I think they let him in because they think he expected us
to say 'no' and he would print that in his column," another
board official said. Mr. Shanker writes a weekly advertisement
in the New York Times stating the union's position on educational issues. The advertisement subsequently carried a further
attack on Dr. Gittell's appointment.

Dr. Gittell called Mr. Shanker's criticism "an outright vio-
lation of my academic freedom." Like board headquarters
officials who backed her up, she said her work in the politics
of education are a part of her work as a political scientist.

She dismissed Mr. Shanker's contention that her scholarly
work was inferior by pointing out that her appointments as a
full professor and her selection as associate provost at Brooklyn
College had been endorsed by her "academic peers" who first
scrutinized and approved her work and publications.

Dr. Gittell had locked horns with the union leader during
the 1968 teachers strike, which was precipitated in large measure
by the insistence of a special school board for the Ocean Hill–
Brownsville district on power to select its own teachers. Dr.
Gittell strongly supported the school board, whose position was
equally strongly opposed by Mr. Shanker and the union.[28]

It is also unlikely that any school administrator who is not
acceptable to the leadership of teachers' organizations can be
hired by a school board. When the candidates for chancellor
of the New York City School District were being reviewed,
one of them being considered explained in confidence that his
name was stricken from the list because he was unacceptable
to the UFT leadership. The person had a strong "public interest" track record as a school administrator.

Two professors, Reginald Damerell and Maurie Hillson,
writing in *Phi Delta Kappan*, charge that the UFT's weekly
advertisement in the New York *Times* misleads the public

[28] January 13, 1974.

with "sophisticated" advertising techniques. The authors accuse the UFT president of using the weekly column to help promote his own power position in the anticipated new national teachers' organization.

As an example of deceptive advertisement, Damerell and Hillson point to the ad of November 26, 1972, headlined "High-Sounding Reforms and Low Reading Scores":

> . . . A further decline in the reading scores of the city schools had just been announced. The ad used the decline to discredit the concept of "decentralization" and the reform ideas of the first chancellor for the newly decentralized system. It was apparent that the TIMES had not reviewed the ad's copy for truthfulness. Shanker wrote: "[W]e are nearing the completion of the third year of decentralization. . . ." What was nearing completion, at the time, was the THIRD MONTH of that school year. The third year of decentralization was 12 months away. The sentence was false as it stood. It goes on to say, ". . . we should have expected improvement," and reads in such a manner as to indicate that the reading scores were up to the moment, instead of the results of tests given THE PREVIOUS SPRING. The reading scores, in fact, reflected only one year and eight school months of decentralization— not nearly the three years the ad led readers to believe. Actually, in the third year of decentralization, the NEW YORK TIMES (September 26, 1973) reported an overall gain in reading achievement.[29]

In other places, organized teachers' groups take an active role in electing school board members who are sympathetic to their interests. In one case, the board member was elected so that he could lead a "dump the superintendent" movement against a superintendent who had taken a hard line against relinquishing any policy decisions to the teachers. A suc-

---

[29] "The UFT Tells It Like It Isn't and Makes It Look Like It Is," *Phi Delta Kappan*, Vol. LV, No. 6, February 1974, pp. 380–81.

cessful "election" enabled the teachers to have this superintendent placed in exile in the school system itself.

In New Jersey the state teachers' association helped oust the state education commissioner. Recognized as one of the leading national educators, Dr. Carl Marburger was accused by the teachers' association of undermining the rights and privileges of teachers. The New York *Times* had this to say about the case:

> In voting down the reappointment of Education Commissioner Carl L. Marburger, the New Jersey State Senate has surrendered to pressure by the conservative education establishment and the anti-busing constituency. The rejection of a forward-looking leader in a field overstocked with the unimaginative bureaucrats is a harsh blow to the public education system of a state that has only recently begun to catch up with modernity.
>
> Dr. Marburger's narrow defeat is being hailed as a victory by the powerful New Jersey Teachers Association. Since the Commissioner was opposed for his support of both integration and educational reforms, this represents a sorry triumph for an association constantly seeking to project a progressive image for itself. It is ironic that the association never even attempted to invoke against Dr. Marburger's ultra-conservative predecessors the kind of political action that helped to defeat a commissioner who had won state and national acclaim as an able and effective educator.
>
> The Senate's irresponsible action is being interpreted as a blow to Governor Cahill who nominated Dr. Marburger and considered him a trusted education aide. Sadly for New Jersey, it is a defeat that speaks better for the Governor than for his "victorious" opponents.[30]

In New York City noted educational reformer Dr. Harvey Scribner left after nearly three years as the first chancellor of the New York City public school system. Some observers be-

[30] New York *Times*, September 11, 1973.

lieve that he fell victim to status quo forces which included the UFT. For example, A. H. Raskin makes the following observation on this very point:

> The central board brought in a new Chancellor three years ago to revitalize the shattered system in the wake of Ocean Hill. That Chancellor Dr. Harvey Scribner, a champion of decentralization as an avenue for involving black and Puerto Rican parents in better education for their children, has now been forced out of office, in large measure a victim of persistent UFT hostility.
>
> With Scribner gone, the old line school bureaucracy has been reorganized from within, thus entrenching under the guide of "new blood" the kind of old blood the union likes best.[31]

In an unusual case the AFT sued Simon and Schuster, the publisher of the book *Teachers and Power: The Story of the American Federation of Teachers*, by Robert Braun.

This book presented a critical exposé of the AFT as an organization seeking to control the public schools. The AFT threatened a libel suit in the amount of seven million dollars if the book were not restricted. In a series of articles, the well-known author and reporter for the *Village Voice* Nat Hentoff challenged Simon and Schuster on the grounds that it had abandoned production of the controversial book in an attempt to settle the suit with the AFT. Given his assessment of the issues surrounding this case, Hentoff expresses his central concern:

> Simon & Schuster's silence in the face of a suit clearly intended to stifle a book with the attendant "chilling effect" of that silence on other writers who might write critically of the AFT utterly ignored the first amendment issues in this case. . . .[32]

[31] "Shanker's Great Leap," *New York Times Magazine*, September 9, 1973.
[32] The *Village Voice*, December 28, 1972.

Of course, there is the whole other side of this case; i.e., the causes that promoted the AFT libel suit included claims of inaccuracies and biased reporting. (Braun's book was a personal account and not a "scholarly" history of the AFT.) Simon and Schuster reported that they did not "suppress" the book, but that it was not selling—that it simply was not a successful commercial venture.

Regardless of the varying positions, it seems clear that the UFT has the clout that can serve as a powerful deterrent to foundations, publishers, writers, academicians, and reporters who may basically challenge the teachers' unions, its agenda and tactics. This deterrent capacity, which is a legitimate weapon given the political power arena of the schools today, is nevertheless suppressive. Ironically, the teachers who rose to power on the issue of teacher oppression have now possibly reversed roles.

In the spring of 1970 and 1973, new community school board elections were held under the New York City School Decentralization Law of 1969. Under this act, community school board elections are much the same as any political election. No special provision is made to guarantee parent representation on community school boards. In other words, the elections are thrown open to the normal political processes which favor organized groups. During the 1970 elections, such organized groups as the Roman Catholic Church, the United Federation of Teachers, and antipoverty agencies assumed active campaigning roles. This continued in the 1973 community school board elections. The UFT assumed a particularly strong role.

Here is how one reporter, covering the local school board elections, saw the situation in the spring of 1973:

> The United Federation of Teachers has been running one of the biggest political campaigns in its history to advance its

favored candidates in this week's community school board elections.

Antipoverty agencies, according to a Community Development Administration official, have been printing leaflets for some community school board candidates, despite rulings by the Office of Economic Opportunity here and in Washington that had barred such activity.

Candidates have been advertising themselves with buttons, leaflets, signs and press releases, hoping to win over voters who will be selecting nine-member boards for the city's 32 school districts. . . .

Although there are fewer candidates involved in this election than in the first, held in 1970, there are more politicians, more antipoverty employees, more teachers-union staff members and altogether more signs of political professionalism this year than there were in the 1970 campaign.

. . . The United Federation of Teachers is backing school-board slates in 30 districts, with the philosophy, recently expressed by the federation president, Albert Shanker, that "in the nineteen seventies bargaining is not enough" to protect the interests of teachers and that "political action is the answer."[33]

The results of these 1973 community school board elections were, therefore, not surprising. The UFT succeeded in getting well over half of its candidates elected to the 234 seats that were vacant. While the United Parents Association was also active in the school elections, it did not do as well as the UFT.

However, it must be recalled that the UFT had opposed the decentralization of the New York City schools. Most of the public utterances concerning community school boards by the UFT were rather pessimistic. However, once the UFT was successful in getting a majority of their candidates elected to these same community school boards, the attitude of the UFT began to change. Thus, at the start of the school year

[33] New York *Times*, April 29, 1973.

in September 1973, the president of the UFT referred to the new community school boards as one of the "hopeful signs" for the school year, saying:

> Last May's elections produced community boards which—most of them—reject confrontation, patronage and separatist ideologies, and which want to cooperate with teachers and the rest of the educational community to improve the schools.[34]

It appears reasonable to assume that the UFT feels better about things because in a sense they have succeeded in capturing control of school decentralization. Once decentralization is made to work for the UFT, it is obviously no longer a negative idea. It is only natural that once a plan moves to your benefit and is no longer threatening to your interests, it becomes acceptable. In the case of the New York City school boards, it seems clear that the UFT's superior fiscal and organizational capabilities gave it a decided edge in the political campaign which surrounded the local elections. Others who were not organized or were only semiorganized were at a definite disadvantage in these elections. However, the UFT victory does not erase the feelings of hostility between teachers and parents—if anything, it may aggravate them. Obviously, this will depend on how the UFT uses its new power base.

Meanwhile, United Parents Association in New York City made the following assessment of the community school board election:

> Parents were much better organized for this election than in 1970, and the results reflected this preparation. UPA undertook the major educational program for parents on how to organize and win in the election process. Where parents associations agreed on their slate and were more or less unified, there were

[34] New York *Times*, September 10, 1973.

successful campaigns. Parents found it difficult to compete with organized political and wealthy union opposition. The 1973 campaign was characterized by politicalization, polarization, intensified power plays and well-financed professional activity in competition with less sophisticated parent groups with limited funding and less political expertise.[35]

In the meantime, activist parent groups are forming throughout the country. These advocacy-oriented groups often respond to school developments that appear to run counter to the interest of their children. Often the route of collision between parent and teacher can be observed. For example, in Syracuse, New York, the Coalition for Quality Education, a parent-oriented body, came into existence over a negotiation article in the teacher contract dealing with discipline. Under the article, teachers were given the power to use physical force in dealing with students, and to exclude such students at their (the teachers') discretion.

The adoption of this article over the strong protest of the Coalition for Quality Education prompted the parent group to announce a school boycott and the setting up of Freedom Schools. The teachers' association had announced a strike if the article on discipline were stricken from the contract. The Board of Education and the Coalition negotiated a solution that school advisory committees would deal with the problem of discipline.

With this particular crisis past, the Coalition for Quality Education continued to press for other parent-child-centered reforms. However, after such episodes one wonders what gut level feeling remains between parents and teachers.

Naturally, teachers' organizations oppose any legislative attempts that may jeopardize the interests of their members.

---

[35] "Community School Board Elections—1973" (United Parents Associations of New York, Inc., 1973).

The case is crystal clear on the matter of teacher tenure. Once a teacher passes his or her probation period, he or she is entitled to tenure. Tenure protects the teacher from arbitrary or unwarranted dismissal and established academic freedom. Few would argue these rights. However, certain teachers view tenure as guaranteed lifetime employment. Assured of continuing appointment and job security, they tend to fall into patterns of mediocrity. It is extremely difficult to deal with these matters after the granting of tenure. Yet many parents, students, and school administrators know that certain teachers are not producing. Some parents and students go as far as stating that these teachers are "incompetent" and should be replaced. But the legal appeals are extremely complicated. The limited number of teachers whose continuing contract has been terminated attests to the difficulties in dealing with non-productive teachers.

While there are various reasons why inferior teachers have been placed on tenure (the manpower strain imposed by previous decades of teacher shortages and improper evaluation by administrators during the probationary period), the fact remains that many experienced teachers are not enhancing the learning process with children. These same teachers are protected by teachers' organizations. Since the first set of objectives for any present professional association is to protect its members, the results are against the interests of children and the public.

This point is made clear by the Commission on Public School Personnel Policies in Ohio in its report, "Teacher Tenure":

> The welfare of children must always be considered ahead of the financial or psychological needs of the teacher for a job. Furthermore, hard decisions may have to be made that place the present needs of children ahead of past years of loyal

teacher service. The major consideration in continuing the employment of a teacher should be the teacher's present ability to teach. This approach is essential to the status of the teaching profession as well as the welfare of students.[36]

But teachers' associations would be taking a high risk if they did not protect teachers—whether or not they deserve protecting. The reason is simple: If too many tenured teachers are "terminated for incompetence," it opens the door to others. "I might be next" is the psychology triggered by such efforts, and if the professional association can't protect, what good is it?

During the 1960s, the war on poverty stimulated new careers for the poor in the field of education. The creation of so-called paraprofessional positions in schools enabled community residents, some of whom had not completed high school, to assume roles inside the schools. Many of the paraprofessionals handled noninstructional roles such as lunchroom duty or clerical assistance; others began to assume more responsible functions such as maintaining classroom discipline. Since many of the paraprofessionals came from the same background as many of the students, they were more able to "speak their language."

As these community-based personnel became accustomed to the school system, they soon began to see that many teachers in ghetto schools were not able to keep the children occupied with the curriculum. In certain quarters of the community, they discovered that teachers could not control the children and that, therefore, little learning was taking place. Certain teachers were classified as "weak." In some areas, parents complained about the teachers and placed pressure for their transfer. Some paraprofessionals explained that even

---

[36] "Teacher Tenure," *The Second Report of the Commission on Public School Personnel Policies in Ohio*, September 1971, p. 3.

without a college background, they were doing as well as some of the experienced teachers.

These incidents helped create the growing mood in the minority communities that there were teachers who were not teaching, but who were collecting paychecks nonetheless.

Legislatures responding to the public call for increased educational productivity have attempted to lengthen the probationary period preceding tenure. In New York State, for instance, the legislature passed a five-year probationary period. The UFT of New York City almost immediately negotiated a contract in 1972 which reduced the probationary period to three years.

Further attempts to deal with increased educational productivity by focusing on experienced teachers are similarly opposed by professional teachers' groups. Some states are now considering a new type of licensing procedure for teachers called competency-based certification. The attempt here is to require all new teachers to demonstrate successful performance with children as the major indicator of competence, rather than successful completion of college courses. The aim is to have licensed only those teachers who have exhibited professional competencies with children.

At present, both undergraduate teachers in training and experienced teachers in the schools attend colleges and universities to take courses that are intended to develop these competencies.

A teacher may get good grades in these courses, but there is no way of knowing whether this will really make any difference in the classroom with children. The feeling is growing among school administrators, parents, and school boards that an accumulation of college courses is no guarantee of increased competence in the classroom.

With more pupils falling behind in basic skills, with high

physical and psychological dropout rates, with high absentee-ism, discipline problems, boredom, etc., it is difficult to see what, if any, real difference accumulated course credits make.

Yet today it is exactly the number of course credits that indicates the attainment of increased levels of professional achievement. Teachers are rewarded with increments in salary when they earn greater numbers of college credit. Thus, a bachelor's degree plus thirty hours entitles a teacher to one salary and a bachelor's plus sixty entitles a teacher to a higher salary.

Naturally, the assumption undergirding such teacher salary schedules is that the more college credits one has, the better he is with children. However, the real criterion for being better is whether pupils are learning. When such a correlation is attempted—when an entire grade school or school district is evaluated in terms of the relationship between teacher level on the salary scale and student learning—the assumptions behind the salary schedule break down.

Therefore, state education agencies are trying to provide periodic assessments of the experienced teacher, including tenured teachers—based on their actual performance with children—as a requirement for maintaining a teaching license. Obviously, this is enormously threatening to classroom teachers, and teachers' organizations mobilize to defeat any such mandates. Certainly, teachers have some justifiable concerns with such assessments, but the real motivation for teachers' organizations not to help state departments of education to develop solid procedures which get at teachers who are incompetent concerns their primary role of protecting teachers. As organizations, they must demonstrate to the rank and file that they are strong enough to save all teachers.

As an example, in New York State, the State Education Department is establishing a new standard for teacher certification based on performance with children rather than course completion. The popular name given to this procedure is Competency Based Teacher Certification. An essential feature of this new statewide licensing plan is co-operative governance at the regional level. Under this plan no teacher preparation program will be accredited by the State Education Department that does not have the signature of (1) the chief executive of the institution of higher education, (2) the school district administrator of participating school district(s), (3) the professional staff representatives, and (4) representatives of other relevant agencies.

The New York State Union of Teachers took a strong position opposing the new certification. Once it appeared that the State Department of Education would continue to press forward on this licensing plan, the union adopted the strategy that the *local bargaining agent* would have to be included on any local governance package. That is to say, no local teacher preparation program would be accredited by the state that did not carry the signature of the local teacher bargaining agent. The local bargaining agent is a direct affiliate of the New York State Union of Teachers who is elected locally and who represents teachers on *all* matters. The bargaining agent takes his signals from the policies established by the state teachers' union.

The insistence that any state plan approved by the New York State Commissioner of Education carry the local bargaining agent led to considerable debate. Finally, New York State Commissioner Ewald Nyquist issued the following ruling:

> As a result of the April 13, 1973, Regents Advisory Board Invitational Conference the matter of designating the bargaining agent as the official representative of the professional staff in competency based, field-centered teacher education programs

has been laid before the Commissioner. He has subsequently made clear that he feels it inappropriate for the Department to mandate for the purpose of teacher preparation, the school's bargaining agent although he feels that the teachers should clearly be represented by someone selected by the teachers. If the bargaining agent were so mandated, for instance, the direction of the teacher education program could become a part of negotiations and such a relationship unnecessarily could confuse the collaboration sought in programs for the preparation of teachers.[87]

The strong influence of the state teachers' union finally resulted in a compromise statement in the application material which was used for submitting new proposals for teacher education programs. An asterisk after "the professional staff representative(s)" refers to a footnote which explains, "It is suggested that a representative of the recognized professional association be the representative of the professional staff. The professional staff representative or representatives may not be appointed by either the school district administration or the institution of higher education."

It is clear that if the bargaining agent is not represented on the local board level, then the co-operation of teachers could not be guaranteed. In fact, without such representation, unionized teachers would resist any program advanced under this new plan. Since no new certification program can work without teacher co-operation, this threat to withdraw teacher participation, if carried out, would guarantee the failure of competency-based licensing. On the other hand, if the bargaining agent were included, then considerable power in the licensing of teachers would be in the hands of the union. The bargaining agent, as a bona fide member of a statewide team of unionized teachers, would carry out policies determined by

[87] Memorandum from Vincent G. Cazzetta, Director, Division of Teacher Education and Certification, State Education Department.

central union headquarters. These policies are intended to protect teachers from a number of conditions, including extra work. Obviously, regional boards set up to oversee the development of a new approach to the certification of teachers cannot get very far without altering the status quo. To implement competency-based teacher education would require a redefinition of the role of the teachers who participate. It may require that students in teacher preparation who are at different stages of development spend more time in the field (field-centered teacher preparation), that is, in certain public schools. Experienced teachers in such schools are expected to spend more time helping to guide and prepare these students. Some students may be working as "aides," others as "assistants," still others as "interns." This type of differentiation changes the working conditions of experienced teachers. They are now supervisors of preservice teachers. These schools need to become converted into "lighthouse" centers that exemplify the best environments for children. Experienced teachers must spend time planning and developing new programs. When will the teachers in these centers have time to plan? Will they be paid extra for this extra service? Who will pay for such extra service?

The State Department of Education is expecting that this new state certification will be implemented from current expenditures. The state legislature, feeling the crunch of public accountability in education, has not made new moneys available for the implementation of competency-based teacher certification. Consequently, it is reasonable to assume that after the preliminary period of stated co-operation among the basic parties in the local governance team, there would be a period in which substantive changes would be proposed. It is during this period that the bargaining agent would begin to raise questions, begin to check back with central union officials, assume a stance of protecting teachers from any redefined roles and responsibilities unless this were accompanied by more money. After all, the argument could be made that any new developments affect the teachers' working conditions and thus the negotiated contract. After a while, the bargaining agent would begin to veto most substantive proposals that required the teachers to redefine their roles. Moreover, if teachers did participate they would be spending time in extra duties requiring extra money. Either the state or the local school boards would have to pick up the tab, thereby subjecting both to unexpected fiscal strain.

We have caught other glimpses of the potential political power of unified teachers. For instance, in Bangor, Maine, during the summer of 1972 the teachers' association rebelled against the education courses offered by the School of Education at the University of Maine. The teachers boycotted the summer program. They did not enroll, and the low enrollments were causing serious financial consequences for the university.

If teachers were to implement boycott policies emanating from their state or national union, they could bring not only public schools to a halt, but teacher preparation institutions as well. Teacher education is the bread and butter of many colleges and universities. Thousands of teachers in the field must acquire advanced graduate courses in education in order to maintain and/or sustain state certification. These courses are offered by departments of education within institutions of higher education. Almost all institutions of higher education depend upon enrollments to sustain their operations.

Often students enrolled in education make up the bulk of the support for other services offered by the college or university. If teachers were to stop attending these education courses, the consequences to higher education could be devastating.

Further, if the teachers' union were to claim (as it has begun to) that courses in education are unrelated to the needs of classroom teachers and that the teachers' union through teacher centers could do the job better, then teacher education itself would be transferred to its over-all control.

It must be made clear that one of the major agenda items for any profession is to control entry into the profession itself. Teacher control of teacher education would accomplish this. The strategy of the New York State Union of Teachers appears to be to capture the governance of the new competency-based certification process, thereby controlling one of the essential features to professional entry. With such an achievement under their belts the other ingredients to take control of *entry* would not be far from their grasp.

Another important feature in entry control is the teacher centers—teacher-directed units which have arisen in England and which evidently perform successful social functions. They also provide opportunities for teachers to meet informally to compare educational ideas.

Since teacher centers are designed by teachers for teachers, they are becoming popular in this country as well as in England. Some observers believe that teacher centers can become the major vehicle for improving education. One strong advocate is the president of the UFT:

> Our schools of education, from which most of the writing on method has flowed, suffer from an institutional disadvantage, they are too far removed from the classroom, the place where education takes place. This is certainly one of the reasons for teachers' complaints that their education courses do not help them very much in dealing with day-to-day classroom problems.

In theory such daily guidance should be provided by the supervisors to whom the teachers are assigned. But supervisors generally are too preoccupied with their own tasks and concerns (parental complaints, authorization of purchases and repairs, student disorders, and what not) to provide much supervision. Moreover, teachers are reluctant to request supervision since this might be interpreted as an admission of inadequacy. In the end, teachers by and large are left to their own devices in developing ways to teach children effectively. Some succeed; others do not.

A model system for improving teacher performance now exists in England in the form of more than 500 teachers' centers functioning throughout the country.[38]

It is not difficult to consider that if teacher centers could become the focal point for the new state system of certification, entry into the profession could be controlled by the union. Since the essential ingredient of teacher centers is teacher control and since the bargaining agent represents teachers on all matters, it is not difficult to decide the broader political strategy. Teacher centers can indeed make an important contribution to reform. However, both the control and the direction of the reform could be decided by a centralized teachers' union policy.

By appealing to the commonsense, practical value of teacher centers, the image is established with the public and the classroom teachers that this new idea can help solve basic educational problems where all else has failed. Almost all educators would agree that no reform is possible without teacher participation. Unless classroom teachers are a part of any development, can understand and believe in the directions being taken, then no real change is possible. However, there

[38] "Teachers' Centers: A Needed Educational Reform," from "Where We Stand," New York *Times*, July 22, 1973.

is a difference between teacher participation and teacher control as provided by a professional union. It is clear from the New York State experience with competency-based teacher certification that the issue is not participation but control. By insisting that the bargaining agent be the key participant, and not teachers who may be elected by classroom teachers specifically for the program being considered, the agent of the union takes priority. To insist that the bargaining agent represent teachers on *all* matters forecloses any alternative route to teacher involvement. Bargaining agents are first of all union-oriented—they are part of the statewide team. Classroom teachers may not have this union orientation with all of its political know-how. Classroom teachers may only be interested in educational matters. They may participate with others solely on the basis of what makes sense educationally—not politically, i.e., not in terms of what is best for the union. There is a basic difference between teachers and teacher union.

Thus, classroom teachers may agree to matters that do not give priority to union interests. Classroom teachers may be elected by their peers on the basis of talents in supervision or curriculum—that is to say, in educationally substantive matters. However, such criteria are unacceptable to a statewide teachers' union. Its task is unification through standardization. It needs a well-disciplined body of teachers in order to maximize its political clout. It would not be to its best interest to have a group of well-intentioned teachers agree to conditions that would later compromise the union's across-the-board bargaining ability.

To achieve reform classroom teachers selected randomly may agree to meeting after school for certain activities, to differential staffing, to larger classes on occasion, to supervising student teachers without pay, and to a host of other items that would pose serious problems for the union during the collective bargaining. In fact cases have been reported in which teachers of a school wanted to participate in a competing based program involving a local teacher preparation college but were overruled by the teachers' association which was, in turn, responding to signals from the central state teachers' headquarters.

By having the bargaining agent represent teachers on *all* matters such problems can be obviated. Further, bargaining agents can accept the ultimate goal of union control. With competency-based teacher certification, this means controlling the process by which new teachers are licensed. In short—control over *entry* into the teaching profession.

In power terms, the teachers are the strongest members of any governing board. If the bargaining agent represents teachers on any governing board for competency-based licensing of teachers, for example, then he can veto any items that run counter to union interests. A veto could mean that teachers would be given orders not to participate, and without teachers nothing can go forward. This means that the other members of the governing board are always at the mercy of the union representative. Since the other members do not have the same command of power, we have a governing board composed of unequals. Slowly, by virtue of its superior power, the union will control the governing board and thus the policies overseeing the licensing process. Slowly, the direction will be toward teacher centers. This will mean that teacher preparation itself will be turned over to teachers' unions. The monopoly would be complete.

Thus, while teachers' organizations get stronger, the schools themselves do not improve. In fact, teachers' organizations seem to get tougher in the large city system, which are caught in a decline in quality. An inverse relationship seems to exist between teacher militancy and the quality of the schools; i.e., the higher the militancy, the lower the quality. This cycle is not difficult to understand. With a decline in quality comes consumer protest which, in turn, stimulates the unification of those criticized. As usual, parents and citizens demand that everything be done. This places critical pressure on teachers to resist these outside threats by sticking together, behind their professional association. Since the AFT has emerged as the tougher of the two major teacher organizations, its stance gains in appeal with city schools (most AFT affiliates are in cities, e.g., New York, Philadelphia, Newark, Washington, Detroit).

However, what started out as demands from city parents and citizens is spreading into affluent suburbs. Teachers who once accepted the stance of the NEA are now facing the same public pressures as their colleagues in public schools. The hard, tough negotiating skills of the AFT begin to make much sense to teachers. They now realize that their jobs are at stake.

To be sure, it is not surprising that discussions of merger are in process. To many, the New York State Union of Teachers is a breakthrough, pointing the way to similar mergers in other states. By combining forces, teachers' organizations will be more prepared politically to deal with the public pressures.

In this natural process, the integration of these organizations will most likely be a joint enterprise at first, with co-presidents. But as the advanced skill and appeal of the AFT strategy takes hold, the AFT leadership will quickly emerge. The president of the strongest AFT local in New York City appears destined to lead a "United Teachers of America." Or will he?

What has been heralded by the UFT as a model for national teacher unity—namely the New York State United Teachers' merger—held a conference in Canada which revealed some of the same problems inherent in the NEA-AFT strains. The report from the meeting raises some of the underlying dissatisfactions:

> . . . in caucuses that went on long into the night yesterday, and in endless parliamentary squabbles on the floor today, a sizable number of teachers talked of their frustration and bitterness over what they described as domination of the organization from New York City.
>
> John Buscemi, a delegate from Beacon, said, "It's terribly obvious that what has occurred is not a merger but a take-over. We're not a merged organization—we're a captured one."
>
> Some of the complaints focus on specific policies or aspects of the organization's structure. Others are more concerned with attitudes. But what is clear is that merger—despite the green and white "unity" buttons that many delegates sport on their lapels—has not erased and has in some cases exacerbated the long-standing strains and tensions between the philosophies represented by the two original organizations.

The Dissidents' View

The dissident delegates, most of whom are from upstate and from locals that were formerly part of the State Teachers Association, said that they resent the concentration of authority in the hands of Mr. Shanker and Thomas Y. Hobart, the state president who is closely allied with Mr. Shanker, even though before merger he was the president of the State Teachers Association.

The important committee assignments, the dissidents contended, go to former United Teachers members or to Teachers Association members who support the UFT. "The trouble with the leadership is that they think there are only five people in the state with brains enough to run this organization, and that's ridiculous," said David Rightmyer, a delegate from Spackenkill.

"We find ourselves involved in a political machine, and everyone knows that over a period of time political machines breed graft, corruption, and apathy," said Edward J. Robisch, director of the delegates from the five-county mid-Hudson area.

One issue that arose yesterday, the second day of the four-day meeting, seemed to symbolize the conflict. The leadership recommended that the union, now organized as a not-for-profit corporation, should unincorporate to be free under the law to use dues money for activities on behalf of political candidates.

Some delegates, both in public and private, questioned the leadership's motives and said they did not want a small group directing the political use of what could be a large sum of money.

The amendment to unincorporate passed by a vote of 987 (136 more than needed) to 186. The dissidents contended that debate had been cut off before they could bring more of their supporters to the floor for the vote.

"All they needed was a one-third vote to keep the debate open, and they couldn't even get that," Mr. Shanker commented later. "They were simply outvoted."

Views Collide

The dissidents conceded that their own political organization had been minimal and that they were almost always outmaneuvered in parliamentary debate. But they say they value an open structure and have no desire to emulate the strict discipline of the United Federation of Teachers, which makes the New Yorkers so effective on the floor.

Time after time in votes on structural amendments today, delegates rose to warn of the "consolidation of power in the hands of a few people."[39]

Perhaps sensing some of the tactics attributed to the UFT, and realizing the important role that this local chapter plays in the AFT, the negotiating team from the NEA broke off

[39] "Teachers Union Meets in Canada," New York *Times*, March 24, 1974.

merger talks in early 1974. The major issue of whether the
AFT would remain an affiliate of the AFL-CIO could not be
resolved. The NEA advocated an independent unified teaching profession. Rather than adjust to the AFL and its agenda,
the NEA made the conditions the other way around.

The decision to stop further talks of merger elicited a
column in the UFT paid column advertisement in the New
York *Times* which read in part:

> Those who believed that merger was inevitable were also
> looking at the achievements of teachers in New York State.
> Until 1972, New York's teachers had been divided—like their
> colleagues elsewhere—between a warring association and union.
> Despite the years of hostility and despite warnings that rural
> and suburban teachers would never accept AFL-CIO affilia-
> tion, the two organizations DID merge; and the NYS United
> Teachers has been spectacularly successful. One evidence is its
> membership growth. The merged group boasts 25,000 more
> members than the COMBINED TOTAL of its predecessors
> two years ago—or 205,000 members in all.

> That precedent suggested that a national merger would not
> merely have linked the separate memberships of the AFT and
> the NEA, but would have attracted many of the 1.5 million
> teachers who now belong to neither national organization. The
> outcome could have been a national teachers union with 3
> million or more members. The number alone is impressive; but
> the power and influence of such an organization would have
> claimed members in every political election district in the na-
> tion.

> However real these considerations, the media overlooked the
> simplest reality of all: The fact that a given course of action is
> intelligent and reasonable does not make it inevitable.

> And last week the irrational happened—and the hopes of
> teachers all across the country were shattered—as the National
> Education Association abruptly and unexpectedly broke off the
> merger talks.

> Unfortunately, very little of substance had transpired at the

negotiating table; the two sides were only just beginning to get to the issues; the NEA didn't really give teacher unity a chance. . . .[40]

Yet the trend toward teacher unification is still very much alive. Perhaps the "differences" which are surfacing between the NEA and AFT can have a positive effect on the unification movement. Perhaps their "difficulties" will occasion a sober inventory of what the broad aims of unification really are.

There are critically important problems facing public education that require sensitive handling. Among the most pressing is the talk of updating our public system of education so that it can respond to the contemporary aspirations of our pluralistic society.

We desperately need intelligent guidance of the differing demands being projected onto our public schools—demands that, if neglected, can take us dangerously close to stricter uniformity.

We need professional organizations that can liberate the talent of the thousands of dedicated teachers and other school professionals who are eagerly waiting for a force that can harness their good will. Teachers' organizations can be this new force that can channel the constructive energies not only of teachers but of their natural allies, parents and students.

Teachers' organizations can become not only the legitimate protector of professional educators and their academic professional structures and their academic freedom, but that of the citizen as well at the public interest. Teachers' organizations can reorder their priorities, can make the welfare of children the primary operational principle, can become an

[40] "Teacher Unity: Present Hopes Dashed . . . ," from "Where We Stand," New York *Times*, March 3, 1974.

agency which is unsurpassed in its dedication to child advo-cacy.

But this is down the road—at present we must recognize that the structure in which we are performing does not fulfill this function. Our first lesson is to take inventory of the forces that are shaping us. This will require statesmanlike leadership from all quarters, especially from our teachers' as-sociations.

Meanwhile at present, as teachers' organizations grow in power, they will negotiate for more and more authority in controlling the schools. The major areas of policy deal with money and people.

On the fiscal side, teachers' salaries already make up as much as three fourths of all school budgets. Teachers' organ-izations will continue to negotiate for increased across-the-board salary increases, which pleases every member. Attempts on the parts of parents and school boards to reward teachers according to merit, i.e., on the basis of how well they perform with kids, will be defeated. Such policies are divisive to teach-ers' organizations. The leadership would have to deal with serious internal disturbance, morale problems, and the like. Teachers in this system would rather all be treated alike than have their ranks differentiated according to level of actual competency.

Unions would also determine how money is to be spent. Here the track record seems clear. The demands would be for smaller classes, extra help for teachers, more remedial teachers to help children, better facilities, etc. These would carry the rationale that instruction would improve if these things were done.

For example, "performance contracts" in which school boards enter into a contract with private business firms to deliver instructional services, with money-back guarantees, are threatening to teachers. If school boards can do this, then it is possible that most teachers could lose their jobs.

The fact that these proposals are made in desperation, that they reflect the urgent need for reform, goes unattended. Teachers inside the system react to proposals from the point of view, "What will this do to me?"

These proposals seem both unrealistic and threatening. Reality to teachers means facing up to the conditions as they see them in the schools. To them, it makes absolutely good sense to ask for more money to do the following:

1. reduce class size
2. start new classes for nonadjusting students
3. hire more support staff for reading, guidance, school psychology, home workers, etc.
4. hire aides to take care of nonprofessional duties, e.g., lunchroom duties
5. purchase materials that make contact with students

These are the demands that teachers' organizations have attempted to justify.

The More Effective Schools program developed by the AFT has satisfied many of the reality demands of teachers. Invariably, the teachers report great satisfaction in these schools —as do many parents and students. However, as far as whether more scholastic achievement results, the evidence is not conclusive. Yet at each negotiating session the UFT and school board deal with the quality of MES. In the 1972 negotiations in New York, this item was tabled.

More Effective Schools is a compensatory, add-on approach to school improvement. Not only is the MES strategy costly, but the results are questionable. Similar compensatory

efforts have been seriously questioned by the President of
the United States in his education message of 1970:

> The best available evidence indicates that most of the com-
> pensatory education programs have not measurably helped poor
> children catch up.
>
> Recent findings on the two largest such programs are par-
> ticularly disturbing. We now spend more than $1 billion a year
> for educational programs run under Title I of the Elementary
> and Secondary Education Act. Most of these have stressed the
> teaching of reading, but before-and-after tests suggest that only
> 19% of the children in such programs improve their reading
> significantly; 13% appear to fall behind more than expected;
> and more than two-thirds of the children remain unaffected—
> that is, they continue to fall behind. In our Headstart program,
> where so much hope is invested, we find that youngsters en-
> rolled only for the summer achieve almost no gains, and the
> gains of those in the program for a full year are soon matched
> by their non-Headstart classmates from similarly poor back-
> grounds.[41]

During his second term, President Nixon continued to express similar concerns—namely, that federal aid to education
has not been used effectively. Note, for instance, his position
on education as expressed in his message to Congress in September 1973:

> Total Federal outlays for education will reach $13.8-billion
> under my 1974 budget proposals—an increase of $4.8-billion
> over the 1969 level.
>
> Of crucial importance is whether those funds are being
> channeled in such a way as to purchase maximum educational
> benefit for the students they are intended to help.
>
> The experience of nearly a decade since the Federal Govern-
> ment shouldered a major school aid role under the Elementary

---

[41] 91st Cong., 2d sess., Document No. 91-267, House of Representatives, March 3, 1970, p. 5.

and Secondary Education Act of 1965 indicates that these funds are not being used as effectively and equitably as they should be.

However, the issue of class size, next to salaries, is possibly the leading agenda item for negotiations.

Yet studies on smaller class sizes do not point to improved learning. For instance, on the critical problem of teaching reading to inner-city children, the studies conducted by the prestigious Council for Basic Education in Washington, D.C., concluded:

The factors that seem to account for the success of the four schools studied are strong leadership, high expectations, good atmosphere, strong phonics, individualization, and careful evaluation of pupil progress. On the other hand, some characteristics often thought of as important to school improvement were not essential to the success of the four schools: small class size, achievement grouping, high quality of teaching, school personnel of the same ethnic background as the pupils' education, and outstanding physical facilities.[42]

A teachers' union must assume a collective philosophy in the name of equality even if this results in unequal education for children and parents.

It has been the collective philosophy advanced by school people that has resulted in an add-on system of trying to improve our schools which may only result in limited learning payoff to children, but has produced a system of vested interest in the add-on itself. That is to say, as a new layer was added to the old, new people were hired. Those employed naturally developed a vested interest in keeping the program going, whether or not kids were being helped.

[42] "Inner-City Children Can be Taught to Read: Four Successful Schools," *Occasional Papers*, No. 18 (Council for Basic Education), p. 30.

Much of the federal moneys were used in ghetto schools. Jobs created in these settings often went to those in the community who needed work. The abandonment of such programs could result in serious economic consequences for those involved. The thrust is to keep them operational, regardless of the results.

In other situations, teachers were paid at an hourly rate to teach basic skills in after-school programs. The result appeared to be that those who could not teach during the day, but were getting paid for it, were now being paid again for the afternoon and evening.

Further, negotiated contracts restrict the number of professional meetings teachers may attend after school hours, usually 3:00 P.M. Many school administrators who want to schedule "staff development" meetings after 3:00 P.M. find that they cannot, unless teachers volunteer or are paid extra. The result is fewer staff development meetings that are intended to increase educational productivity.

On a broader scale, teachers who were not adequately prepared to teach in urban schools by preparatory institutions are engaged in the process of gaining advanced preparedness in these same institutions. The result to many is fiscal waste and poor educational productivity.

Yet this is the way the present system works. Putting more money into this type of system will only result in making an old system better—but it remains an old system. At one time, schoolmen were asked to "hide" the shortcomings of the system through planned public relations. Now the shortcomings are becoming so blatant that they defy public camouflage.

Again, through no one's fault, the natural institutional forces impinge on teachers in today's schools, making them move in these self-interested ways. It is altogether natural. The point is that while teachers have a strong rationale for these actions, it is based on their needs, given the existing structure of education—a structure that has never really placed the children first.

On personnel policies, teachers' unions will have more to say in terms of who gets hired in education. Teachers will gradually select principals and school superintendents. Obviously, their selections will be based on how sympathetic the candidate is to teacher demands. If an administrative candidate were to speak in favor of increased parent participation, or believed in teacher accountability, he would be a choice suspect. If a board of education attempted to hire a procommunity candidate who took a hard stand on teacher evaluation based on competence, who would differentiate teachers according to talent and style, he would not likely receive union approval. A board of education would have difficulty hiring a person over union disapproval given the power that teachers would wield. Teachers could strike and at least sabotage any educational movement if such a person were hired against the strong opposition of union leadership.

Most importantly, we have suggested that teachers' organizations are seeking control of entry into the teaching profession. If they could determine who is qualified to enter, they would be virtually assured of absolute power. They could screen candidates that meet their standards. Obviously, a candidate that is not pro union would be suspect; a person who looks "too good" may make others in the ranks look too bad in comparison.

Faculty power in matters of personnel selection are already strong in higher education. One prominent Ivy League dean voiced opposition to this move toward faculty control of entry. He related an incident in which the faculty opposed his candidate for a position. Overriding faculty opposition, the dean did hire the person, who went on to win a Pulitzer prize.

We have indicated that teachers' unions operate better when all teachers are viewed as the same. Obviously, an attempt to differentiate teachers according to some ranking related to how well learning is taking place is to be avoided. Many school boards, in an attempt to reward good teaching, to motivate others to good teaching, to increase educational productivity, have proposed differentiated staffing. Differentiated staffing has many faces, but usually it is tied to merit pay, i.e., rewarding competent teachers with a different salary and rank. For example, some have proposed that their teachers who are demonstrating outstanding performance be called master teachers and be given a regular salary increment.

If this were done, then other educational personnel could be ranked—such as teacher, teacher associate, teacher assistant, teacher aide, each rank revealing a certain stage of competence and commanding a proportionate salary.

However, such differentiation ran against the interest of teachers' organizations. Such plans not only splinter the teachers but also give school boards and administrators important powers that can be used to weaken teacher solidarity. Instead, it makes much more sense for teachers' unions to embrace a policy of all teachers with a bachelor's degree and certification to be viewed as the same. Any differentiation of salary should be based on years of experience and the number of hours of credit taken at a teacher preparation institution. Thus, a teacher with fifteen hours of credit on an established teachers' salary scale gets one salary, the teacher with thirty hours gets more, and so on.

This policy is now accepted by most teachers because it is manageable. That is, taking courses can be troublesome and can also be irrelevant to the professional needs of the teacher, but it is preferable to having some system of classroom performance determine whether a salary increase is forthcoming.

The fact that there has been sharp criticism of the relationships between accumulated course credits and increased student learning is ignored. The 1972 New York City teacher contract solidified even further the course credit policy for determining teachers' salaries.

However, we should be all reminded that as authority flows from the teachers to the unions, the individual teacher finds it more difficult to make his or her own professional decision.

Teachers' unions are becoming centralized agencies with concentrated power at this center. Further they are seeking stark uniformity among its rank and file. Central leadership is perpetuating a sense of sameness among all teachers. This wave of centralization and uniformity speaks against the professional individuality of teachers and their natural diversity.

And while it may be easier for a centralized teachers' union to negotiate with the other centralized agencies on school matters, and while teachers' unions may actually prefer centralized structure for political purposes, such structures are not necessarily good for children, and that is our key concern.

School reform if it is to be achieved will have to break down the highly centralized, uniform and factory-like structures which they encourage. Teachers' unions can maintain a structure that unites teachers without breeding professional uniformity. As we shall suggest later, it is possible for teachers' unions to encourage diversity among teachers and their programs.

Nonetheless teachers' organizations have really "caught on" to the way the political ball game is played. American society moves as a result of organized power. Those who are unorganized remain powerless and unable to improve their lot. It is naïve, argue teachers' organizations, to believe that teachers can get results by appealing to the "good will" of those in control. Teachers' salaries would still be scandalously low if they continued to assume a quiet, passive role. They are absolutely correct. The name of the game today in education is power. This is the new politics of education. Teachers have had to assume this new power role in order to get results.

This logic is correct and appropriate—as long as we are talking about salaries. It is a callous person, indeed, who would not want teachers earning a decent wage.

But the exercise of power does not end with wages and working conditions. If we can have our wage demands met, why not demand and get the other things that will make our job easier—smaller and smaller classes, only those students who do the things that we want them to do, shorter hours, more free time, job security, tenure, responsibility to ourselves, control over who comes into teaching and who, if any, gets out—in short, control over the whole business of education. And why not? If we had control, could we do any worse than uninformed laymen or politicians? After all, argue teachers, we are trained professionals—we know our job and we are also committed to kids. If we had control, if we had most of the power, we would use it to do good things. Power will not corrupt us—because we are professional educators.

Unfortunately, this is not the way political power works. Power seeks more power and is halted only when there is a countervailing power force.

If teachers' organizations had the power to control the schools, they would make sure that *their* own needs come first. This is the *natural* thing to do. The *unnatural* thing to do is to give up power or to use it primarily for nonselfish ends.

Therefore, the quest for teacher power is both natural and necessary—to play by the ground rules of contemporary politics and the dictates of an outmoded educational institution. The consequences for playing this type of game are to take away power from those who do not have the organization to compete. This means students and parents—the educational consumers themselves. It is ironic that those for whom the institution exists are the very ones who will be left out of this political scrimmage.

A democratic society cannot allow this to happen. Many educational statesmen have warned that "education is too important to be left to educators." Public schools are just that—public. Because of their intrinsic connection with the schools, parents have a special set of rights and responsibilities. Parents are usually motivated to protect the maximum welfare of their children. As such, they make up an important sector of the public. They need to have a strong policy role in the education of their children. But parents are not really organized to play the power game. Most want to work closely with teachers, most view teachers as allies, and rightfully so.

Braun expresses the disappointment many feel with the directions being taken by teachers' unions:

> Sadly for an organization which has the muscle and the skill to join with students, parents and others concerned with significant reform of education, the A.F.T. has all but betrayed its founding principles, including those articulated by its most prized member, John Dewey. . . .[43]

Teachers' unions cannot represent the public interest because they are too busy dealing with self-interest. But in our society the public interests and needs come first. Policies dealing with money and personnel, along with other policy areas, cannot be relinquished to professional groups.

American society is now beginning to realize that delegating absolute control to professionals is in the long run counter to the public interest. We have seen the quality of health and

[43] *Teachers and Power*, p. 250.

legal services deteriorate and operate against the consumer. We have seen the military exercise its power without adequate public review. Civilian review of all professions is imperative, not as a suppressor of professional skill and talent, but to protect the public from any abuse. After all, it is the public that delegates to each profession a set of powers that can be used to carry out important functions. This represents a public trust. The public trusts the profession to use this delegated authority to carry out important societal functions.

The public not only has the right to review how this trust is being used to further the service of society, but has a responsibility to do so. This is one of the key features of a democracy. In an open society, public institutions belong to the public. When these institutions are responding to the public, there is little concern for power. It is only when the power that has been delegated to the public is used perpetually for selfish ends that the public reserves its right to an accounting and, if necessary, for a recall of that power and trust.

However, the professions have used their power to mount elaborate systems of organization which threaten to be more potent than the public itself. We have entered a period in which we are dangerously close to having institutions like schools serve the professionals, more than they do the consumers.

In the case of our schools, this is especially dangerous. Education is basic to all societal roles. Schools deal with the talents and values of succeeding generations. Who controls the schools can control the future of our society as well.

Participation takes various forms, but because it deals with decision-making, it is political, and because it is political, there are risks. The objectives of participation in our public schools center on educational quality, not on political power.

Risks are enhanced when educational concerns are exploited for political ends. Stated somewhat differently, all participation in educational reform is a legitimate political means toward educational ends.

There have been and will be occasions when this process is deliberately reversed, when participation is seen as an educational means toward purely political ends. There must be safeguards that protect children and that insure that the participants direct their political energies toward genuine educational ends and do not take advantage of the political aspirations or motives of any vested-interest group.

Advocates of political doctrines are suspect as champions of school reform. The major safeguard is to emphasize the rightful role of the individual parent and student in school decision-making, rather than encourage such decisions from organized groups. The individual parent's connection with the learner is intrinsic and primary, and his concern for the child's growth reasonably pure. The individual student's concern is, of course, with his own destiny, the most direct concern of all.

Individual teachers are also legitimate decision-makers. There is a fundamental difference between the *individual* teacher and the teacher as a member of an organized group. The more that the individual teacher can make decisions, the less need for large teachers' unions to speak collectively for teachers on all professional matters.

The fact remains that, at present, no real reform is possible within our public schools without the support of teachers and their professional organizations. Any proposal dealing with change that is not supported by teachers is doomed to resistance, compromise, and failure.

We have seen proposals for reform through school decentralization, vouchers, and performance contracting heatedly resisted by organized teachers' groups. These were resisted and often defeated because the interests of teachers were jeopardized by these plans. In school decentralization, a centralized system is reorganized into a federation of regional districts. In certain places like New York City and Detroit, community boards oversee each of the regional districts. This plan goes against teacher interests in several ways. Teachers' organizations are getting stronger in dealing with *centralized* boards of education and for negotiating system-wide policies. A decentralized structure distributes this authority pattern, making it difficult for a centralized teachers' organization to negotiate with diverse community boards.

Also, by creating new public bodies to govern each district, the authority of the professional is diminished. There are more lay trustees with which the profession must deal.

Consequently, in New York City proposals that would have structured the role of parents in school decentralization were defeated in favor of direct political elections. This modification made it possible for the teachers' organization to mobilize its resources for proteacher candidates.

Each decentralized plan, other than its own, was fiercely criticized and resisted by the United Federation of Teachers. A compromise plan was finally established.

We have already made note of the resistance to education vouchers. If dissatisfied parents could receive tuition to send their children to private schools, this could lead to the destruction of the public schools and must be resisted at all costs.

The tight budgetary period makes more money packages suspect, especially if these are viewed as doing more of the same.

The point must be kept continuously before us that teachers are responding in terms of the existing system. It does make sense to make these demands. The problem, of course, is that too few of us can rise above the day-to-day reality to see that there are other ways of dealing with school improvement. Teachers' organizations cannot embrace proposals that are not connected to the real world of teachers—so they continue to propose add-on proposals like MES.

However, the desperation is growing from a critical mass of public school users. This discontent has triggered a series of major research efforts which have concluded that public schools make little difference to most students. As suggested earlier, much publicity has been given to the Coleman Report, *Equality and Education Opportunities*, and to *Inequality: A Reassessment of the Effect of Family and Schooling in America*, by Christopher Jenks. Both comprehensive studies point to the limited impact of schooling on children.

These studies, coming as they do when communities are trying to cut school costs, make the climate for teachers all the more precarious. Again, they must look to their professional associations for help.

Locals have begun to experience tougher sledding in school board negotiations. Tight fiscal budgets have helped school boards assume a harder stance even when teachers' unions strike. For instance, in 1970 in East St. Louis, Illinois, a long teachers' strike produced few gains for Local 1220, American Federation of Teachers. The terms of the settlement resulted in six hundred striking teachers returning to work without receiving back pay. The teachers lost an estimated million dollars in wages and benefits.

During the strike, certain teachers resigned their jobs with the school system in order to avoid a court order. These teachers were reinstated on two-year probationary status. These teachers, in essence, lost their tenure and were to be evaluated as beginning teachers. Obviously, in this case the union was weakened as this report makes clear:

> This River community's long teachers strike . . . is not expected to be repeated for a long time. Teachers and school board members agree that the settlement contains no benefits for members of American Federation of Teachers, Local 1220.
>
> Under the terms of the settlement, 600 striking members of the local returned to their jobs without receiving back pay or most of their demands. It has been estimated that the teachers lost more than $1 million in wages and benefits. . . .
>
> All have lost seniority and tenure, although some will be eligible for automatic increases ranging from $230 to $800 a year, depending on years of service and educational preparation. The teachers had asked for no pay increases during the strike, and they were given none by the settlement.[44]

In Yonkers, New York, a teachers' strike in late 1971 and early 1972 resulted in limited gains for the teachers' union. The 1,600-member Yonkers Federation of Teachers closed most of the forty-three city schools. But the school board maintained a stern position which apparently gained the support of the parents. The superintendent reported that few parent or citizen complaints on the prolonged strike were registered.

Concerns were voiced that many parents, especially those who were working, had become adversaries of the striking teachers. Many working parents had to stay home with their children, and were caused severe economic strains as a result.

In the long strike in Newark, New Jersey, during the spring of 1971, the settlement produced little, except perhaps face-saving for the Newark teachers' union. However, the eleven-week strike did leave significant portions of the com-

---

[44] New York *Times,* November 29, 1970.

munity—especially in black and Puerto Rican areas—with a bitterness toward the teachers' union.

In New York City the United Federation of Teachers accepted an eleventh-hour settlement which was far more compromising than expected. This negotiation was the first under the city's school decentralization plan. The New York *Times* lead editorial described the settlement in the following manner:

The new teachers' contract provides the first substantial evidence of the constructive role decentralization can play in improving the city's troubled school system.

It would be easy enough to argue that the Board of Education paid a high price in salary increases to get relatively little in the way of better performance by teachers, but such an argument would ignore what is incontestably the most significant aspect of this contract: It marks the first time since the start of bargaining nearly two decades ago that the United Federation of Teachers did not strongarm the board, under threat of strike, into surrendering control over major elements of basic educational policy.

Far from permitting further erosion of the policy-making function, the bargaining team representing the central school system and the community school boards managed to recover a tiny bit of the ground imprudently given away in past negotiations, even though it would be an exaggeration to suggest that the gains in that direction were remotely comparable to those won by the city itself in its recent round of negotiations with the unions in the uniformed services.

Obviously, the "productivity" of a teacher cannot be measured in the same quantitative terms appropriate to evaluating the efficiency of garbage collection. But there has been scandalous abuse by teachers of the paid time they were allowed for "professional preparation"—time often employed in bridge playing, gossip or shopping, and it is a tribute to the pressure exerted by the community boards that the new agreement provides some safeguards against such misapplication of periods that should be used to heighten professional capacity in the classroom.[45]

In Florida a 1968 statewide two-month strike was called by the Florida teachers' association, an affiliate of the National Education Association. The State Board of Education, with strong citizen support, held sternly to a no-compromise stance. The result was a bitter disappointment to the teachers' association. They won little and lost much in the way of strength and prestige.

These and other cases became clear indicators of coming attractions for teachers' organizations unless they strengthen their ranks through affiliation. Merger talks became more necessary at both the state and the national levels; for a collision with the public can be costly unless adequately prepared.

These early collisions between teachers and public already signal to both parties that tougher strategies are necessary. But collisions are costly—since they apparently do little for the children. Can this power game be altered? Is there a way to begin to deal with the problems that will improve the institutions for everyone?

Is it possible to bring about constructive reform of our public schools with a plan which will (1) build on the best of what we already have; (2) gain the support of teachers and their professional organizations; (3) provide a new responsiveness to parents and students; (4) make fuller use of existing resources rather than raising school expenditures? In short a plan is needed that appeals to mutual respect and co-operation. We need a plan that meets the needs of each of the basic parties at interest.

As we have suggested, any proposed reform will have to

[45] September 9, 1972.

deal directly with altering the uniform structure of public education which swims against the natural tide of student diversity while at the same time it will have to be acceptable to the political forces that now embrace public education. On the latter point, the key public is the teacher's organization which, as we have maintained, has assumed much of the authority formerly residing with school boards and school administration. One factor is clear—without the support of classroom teachers no proposed reform, regardless of its merits, has a chance of success.

Is there such a plan? Can we move from the politics of collision to the politics of co-operation?

III

CO-OPERATION:

The Rise of Alternative Public Schools by Choice

THE PUBLIC SCHOOLS OF AMERICA serve 85 per cent of American children. More than fifty million children go to school each day; another ten million go to college. Over two million teachers assume responsibility for these students. The American public spends over ninety billion dollars to make this enterprise go.

A Gallup poll taken in 1972 showed that 60 per cent of the persons surveyed were satisfied with their children's education, 28 per cent were dissatisfied, and 12 per cent had no opinion. A year earlier, the National Education Association conducted a survey in which four teachers in ten thought teaching as a profession was getting worse.

In a 1973 Gallup survey on education,[1] the following question was among those asked: "In recent years, has your over-all attitude toward the *public* school in your community

[1] George H. Gallup, "Fifth Annual Gallup Poll of Public Attitudes Toward Education," *Phi Delta Kappan*, Vol. LV, No. 1 (September 1973), p. 39.

become more favorable or less favorable?" The results by
groups were as follows:

	National totals (1,627)	Children in schools (928)	Public school parents (620)	Private school parents (124)	Profes-sional educators (306)
Attitudes Toward Schools					
Becoming more favorable	32%	25%	42%	31%	39%
Becoming less favorable	36%	38%	31%	46%	41%
No change/ no opinion	32%	37%	27%	23%	20%

As the size of the educational empire expands, i.e., as
more students are required to stay in school for longer numbers of years (compulsory education), the more both parents
and teachers seem to express dissatisfaction—and with ample
justification.

The current structure of schooling determines who gets to
college, who works in what jobs, etc. For most of us, school
determines the chances we will have in life. If we do not
graduate from high school, we will make less than half the
amount of money than if we could graduate from college.
Equally important, the amount of money you earn determines
where you will live and your standard of living, including the
quality of your medical and legal services. It is not surprising,
therefore, that in the 1973 Gallup poll on education only 2
per cent of the parents who have children in either public or
private schools felt that schools were not important to future
success.

In short, schools are crucial to our lives. Perhaps next to
health and safety, education is our most important value.

Since we all want quality education, we look to the schools to provide it. But the schools as they are structured seem unable to provide all of us with what we want. For about 15 per cent of the population, there are the private schools —usually for the wealthy. For the vast majority, it is the public schools that must deliver this quality.

To administer this growing institution, we established a strict hierarchy—from school boards at the top to teacher and student at the bottom. Rules and procedures developed on high found their way down to the teacher and student in their egg-crate classrooms.

We have already suggested that as masses of different children swarmed into this bureaucratic system, they became labeled. That is to say, as children sat in their fixed rows of seats, as they began to respond to the work presented by teachers in front of them, those who did what was expected were classified in one way and those who did not, in quite another. A system of human classification emerged—"bright," "dull," "average," "slow," "underachiever," "deviant," "backward," "deprived." Every student knew where he stood, and parents came to accept the same classifications.

Teachers began to think of children according to their classification. If a class was considered "bright," the teacher would expect more from them. If the class was "slow," then the teacher did not expect much. A system of self-fulfilling prophecies emerged in which the teacher's expectations had a lot to do with how well the student did. For example, slow students learned that the teacher did not expect as much from them and performed accordingly. Students who were taught to work better with their hands, rather than their heads, were placed in vocational education—usually considered terminal; i.e., students in this track could not go on to college.

At certain times, this system of grouping was challenged as undemocratic because it seemed to fall according to socioeconomic class. The higher the socioeconomic level, the more likely that the child would be in the "bright," academically oriented group. The poor children seemed destined for general and vocational tracks.

Grouping pupils according to ability was labeled homogeneous grouping. A newer and more democratic system of grouping was introduced—heterogeneous groups, in which children were grouped randomly. This new system of grouping posed several problems on teachers who presented their work and found a wide range of responses in her class. If she aimed her teaching at the middle range, then the "faster" and "slower" students would suffer. Many parents complained.

As other cultures came into school—black, Puerto Rican, chicano, Indian—the teacher tried to deal with them in this same way. Teachers, unprepared to deal with these culture groups, tried labeling them as "culturally deprived" or "disadvantaged," and the problems grew. The pupils had to remain in school, but the school was organized to deal with students who were the same, not different.

The present system of schooling forces most children to sit quietly for hours, something that is unnatural for them. Imagine if parents had to keep their children sitting in a chair at home for the same length of time each weekend or during summer vacation. Often when children in school rebel against this format, they are labeled "discipline problems" or "disruptive."

Teachers who rebel against this system also become suspect by an administration geared toward making the existing system function as smoothly as possible.

Parents who themselves went through the same system

have come to expect the same thing for their own children. When they do not see this same procedure followed, they tend to think that something is wrong.

The present structure expects all teachers and students to adapt to this standard educational process. Children from different cultural backgrounds, some speaking a different language from English, are, once in school, abruptly asked to relinquish both their language and their culture in favor of English and a type of middle-class culture which the school reflects. This attempt to homogenize diversity leaves many students and parents with negative feelings of self-worth. When a child is forced to relinquish his language, he is giving up the means by which he has determined who he is. Yet the public school, which aspires to maximize individual growth, goes on with these patterns as a natural course.

Teachers—each one different—are also expected to conform. The present public school framework homogenizes both students and teachers. Instead of cultivating diversity by releasing the positive aspects of being different, the present system viewed diversity as unfortunate barriers to homogeneity.

Teachers and students cannot liberate their natural talents, styles, and strengths under such a system. To do so will only result in frustration for all parties. We have all become familiar with the high absentee role among students. But there is also a correspondingly high rate of absenteeism among teachers. The existing system represses both teachers and students.

Pressures began to build from parents, students, and individual teachers. Discipline problems grew, as did absenteeism. Teachers, doing what the structure of the school dictated, began to feel threatened. Students, bored by the approach, began to get into trouble in school. Teachers had to seek special persons as disciplinarians, and today we need police guards.

As a *diverse, pluralistic* population converged on the monolithic school system, there were bound to be problems. Unable to leave school until a certain age, usually sixteen, those who left knew that their chances in life would be perilously reduced. Parents, unable to afford private schools, all realizing the importance of school, began to pressure those on the inside to produce.

The diverse educational consumer wanted quality. The school was unprepared to deliver quality for everyone. The dropout rate is over 35 per cent nationally and closer to 50 per cent in the cities. Absenteeism among students and teachers is rampant in certain areas. Parents increasingly report that their children are "turning off." Discipline problems grow. Young people, not having their needs satisfied in school, look elsewhere—drugs, cars, etc. Others become bitter and force their frustrations on society through antisocial acts. This results in a waste of human resources and also becomes an added fiscal strain on the taxpayer.

Out of this period of growing crisis in American education came not only a flurry of criticism, not only a realization that public schooling was a critically important function, but recognition that reform efforts were essential. Many of the reform attempts were actually acts of desperation occasioned by the growing problems in the schools. Consequently, desegregation, decentralization, and performance-contracting vouchers were all attempted—often imposed—as a desperation remedy necessary for emergency treatment. The dismal track record in these reforms is testimony to problems inherent in school improvement plans that are advanced as across-the-board proposals for reform or as plans that deliberately favor one party over the other. The dismal track records of these trial plans are in part a testimony to the shortcomings of superimposed attempts at reform. Thus, for example, decentralization was viewed by professional educators as an attempt to transfer all the educational power to local communities. This was clearly perceived by them as favoring the community over the professional educator—something that was unfair and, therefore, to be resisted at all costs. Vouchers were also viewed by professionals as an attempt to bypass public schools in favor of private schools.

The only plan that was not resisted by professionals—compensatory education—became the victim of the high cost–low productivity concerns of the taxpayer. That is to say, while compensatory education was welcomed by school people because it was least threatening to them, it did not help enough children improve in scholastic achievement.

Well, where are we? Some proposals are acceptable to professionals, but not to the public; others are okay for the public, but not for the educators. Even the Ford Foundation, which had given away millions for school improvement efforts, reported that after taking inventory of its programs, the results did not warrant optimism for education.

Do we do nothing? Do we hide behind the accomplishments of our public schools, i.e., emphasizing what is right with them? Do we try to ignore the rising discontent with schools as manifest by absenteeism, vandalism, protests, etc., or do we ignore the need for tripling the number of school guards needed in the New York City schools?

Obviously we need a fresh plan for reform—one that brings out the best in people; one that brings the parties of interest together; one that respects the rights and responsibilities of each; one that is not imposed, does not cost more money; one that will increase satisfaction among parents, students, and teachers; one that can provide quality education to a diverse population.

Fortunately, such a reform plan is emerging, which is variously being called alternative schools, alternative education, options in education, public schools of choice.[2] Regardless of its name, the key ingredients are optional learning environment and the right of individual choice for parents, students, and teachers.

Finally, we appear to have a common ground of support —both parents and teachers in agreement on the direction of reform. The extent of this common support was identified in the Fifth Annual Gallup Poll of Public Attitudes Toward Education, which showed that professional and laymen alike gave high marks to alternative schools. The following breakdown, with the question posed in the survey, gives some idea of the acceptability of the alternative schools idea.

> For students who are not interested in, or are bored with, the usual kind of education, it has been proposed that new kinds of local schools be established. They usually place more responsibility upon the student for what he learns and how he learns it. Some use the community as their laboratory and do not use the usual kind of classrooms. Do you think this is a good idea or a poor idea?

	National totals (1,627)	Children in schools (928)	Public school parents (620)	Private school parents (124)	Professional educators (306)
Good idea	62%	62%	62%	61%	80%
Poor idea	26%	24%	28%	27%	15%
No opinion	12%	14%	10%	12%	5%

[2] For an expanded discussion see Mario Fantini, *Public Schools of Choice*, Simon and Schuster, New York, 1974.

From this table it can be seen that professional educators, who are much more familiar with this idea than the general public, give it an even higher vote of approval.[3]

Such reports give us added hope that alternative education can become the common ground upon which both parents and teachers can unite. It is the one reform proposal before us that has so high an approval vote among both teachers and parents. Leaders of parent associations, as well as leaders of teachers' associations, should welcome the opportunity to work together constructively on school reform through optional education. To do otherwise is not only to abdicate responsibility but to contribute to a potentially catastrophic collision.

Out of the crisis in public education emerged thousands of teachers deeply concerned with improving the quality of education, strongly committed to children, and eager to work with parents and students in developing new educational approaches. These teachers themselves constitute a critical mass of new professional educators, concerned not so much with preserving a collective power of self-interest as with getting on with the crucial task of remaking our public schools. They are also members of teachers' organizations, but their orientation is toward genuine reform. They are more likely to accept as right civilian review and control of public schools. This major group in established professional ranks is made up of professionals who want to be held accountable, but in a new system of education which they have helped develop and which brings out the best in them and their students. They are more likely to be flexible, to oppose their own professional organization when necessary, because to them

[3] Ibid., p. 43.

the task of making schools more responsive to the consumer and the professionals comes first.

Since they are members of teachers' organizations, when they do join with parents and students—as they are presently doing in the design of alternative forms of education—they tend to reduce both the concerns and the resistance of any centralized teachers' association. That is to say, when grass-roots teachers engage in the development of educational options, they are already representing the professional—the teachers' organization—in the process of change. The leadership of a teachers' union is less likely to veto such activities, once started, than would have been the case if those proposing changes had sought the support of the teachers' union first. The agenda of a centralized teachers' union and that of grass-roots teachers in dealing with the solution to problems in their schools can be altogether different. With the new professional teachers it is. As bona fide members of a teachers' union, those teachers can do more to enhance the possibilities for avoiding a collision with the public than if they were a separate group. This bold group may actually help save teachers' organizations from themselves by helping to break new professional grounds. These grass-roots teachers in our public schools give their teachers' organization a new mission tied more directly to the public interest.

Many of these teachers are desperately trying to develop alternative approaches, but are in need of support. Many of them relate stories of frustration in their attempts to convince boards of education and school administrators to explore alternative patterns of education. They also report that their teachers' associations do little to help them either.

However, the leadership of both NEA and AFT have not spoken against developing educational alternatives within the framework of public schools. For example, the president of the New York City UFT is reported as saying that parents and children be allowed to "shop around" among public schools so they can choose a style of education that suits them,[4] although later on the president of the UFT began to express concern over alternative schools in his weekly New York *Times* column:

> . . . The way some critics look at it, the alternative schools, by their demonstration of creativity in their circumscribed function, constitute a sweeping repudiation of the traditional bureaucratic school structure and program.
>
> The rationale of such criticism is defective because it ignores the clearly defined raison d'etre of the alternative school, which is to serve the special needs of a certain segment of the student population. Far from being a full-blown alternative to the regular school, it merely offers an improvisational and, in many instances, last-resort alternative program to those students who had failed to respond to conventional schooling. This type of program is a supplement to rather than a replacement for the regular program. . . .[5]

Furthermore, the reaction to the Rochester, New York, proposal to consider alternatives in education has met with considerable opposition from the Rochester teachers' association. The opposition grew to the extent that the front page of the *New York Teacher*, the official publication of the New York State Union of Teachers, carried the headline "Voucher Plan Opposition Grows," referring to the Rochester plan.[6]

It is important that the alternative school movement not be linked to the "voucher" plan. The voucher is being opposed by teachers' groups because this plan appears to favor private schools. However, alternative *public* schools are something else. We already have a voucher system—it is called

---

[4] New York *Times*, February 7, 1971.
[5] New York *Times*, April 23, 1972.
[6] *New York Teacher*, Vol. 14, No. 14 (December 3, 1972).

public schools. What we do not have in the public schools is alternatives.

The president of the NEA, during 1970, indicated:

> As we enter the 70's, all Americans are concerned about the deteriorating quality of life in our large cities and the crisis in urban schools. In this volume, *The Reform of Urban Schools*, Mario Fantini not only presents a penetrating analysis of the urban crisis but also makes concrete suggestions for renewing urban education through a unique design that he calls the public-schools-of-choice system. Fundamentally a plan in which a range of optional school programs would be offered to diverse student groups in every community, the public schools of choice would open up a range of educational opportunity and choice in public schools heretofore available mainly to the privileged patrons of private schools. It is important to note that Fantini is not suggesting a voucher plan. Rather he is calling for new kinds of public schools.[7]

President David Sheldon, speaking at a conference on alternative schools in San Francisco in February 1973, expressed mixed feelings about the alternatives movement. On the one hand, he felt that "plurality in education" was good but that if linked with "vouchers," it could be opposed. Vouchers convey to teachers a plan that favors private over public schools. Sheldon felt that the key to teacher support for alternatives would be early involvement.

Teachers' organizations could assume an important leadership role in bringing teachers, students, and parents together around the common concern for developing alternative forms of education. Teachers who are attracted by the so-called open education or the informal classrooms can join with parents who are seeking such options in any school or school system. Those teachers, parents, and students who

[7] Foreword, *The Reform of Urban Schools* (National Education Association, 1970), p. 1.

prefer a more standard option can also have it. Teachers' organizations could become one of the enabling vehicles for generating this co-operative venture. In so doing, they will be assuming a constructive leadership role in updating the system of public education.

By turning its attention to the system that restricts institutional arrangements, teachers' organizations will concentrate their enormous talent and power on the real problem —a problem to which many parents and students can also rally their power and energy. In this co-operative process of developing educational alternatives based on choice, the rights of each party—teacher, parent, and student—will not be compromised. Instead, putting aside their weapons of war on each other, they will have entered into a different type of negotiation—one based on mutual trust. Power, in this case, is not a negotiable thing used for combat, but the energy needed to construct viable educational options.

Increasingly in recent months the NEA and its state affiliates have been assuming leadership in considering alternative public schools as a sensible and viable approach to contemporary reform. For example, the California Teachers Association (CTA) not only held a major statewide conference on the theme of alternative programs in public school, in February 1974 but played an important role in helping to pass state legislation which could promote such alternatives within the public school of that state. Note the resolution adopted by the CTA State Council of Education October 7, 1973:

ALTERNATIVE SCHOOLS RESOLUTION
C & I Committee—May 19, 1973

WHEREAS, the growing pluralism within our society demands that a plurality of educational options be provided that can begin to satisfy a greater number of families, and

WHEREAS, children have different learning needs, and no single program yet devised can meet all educational needs, and

WHEREAS, conventional schools need a comparative perspective on all facets of their operations which uniquely different options can begin to provide, and

WHEREAS, there currently exists within the public schools a demand for change and total institutional reform, and

WHEREAS, an alternative school is defined as a separate school within a district or separate class group within a school which is organized to:

   (a)   maximize the opportunity for students to develop the positive values of self-reliance, initiative, kindness, spontaneity, resourcefulness, courage, creativity, responsibility, and joy;

   (b)   maintain a learning situation maximizing student self-motivation and encouraging the student to follow his own interests;

   (c)   maximize the opportunity for the students, teachers and parents to continuously react to the changing world, including, but not limited to, the community in which the school is located,

THEREFORE BE IT RESOLVED that CTA encourages and wholeheartedly supports the use of educational alternatives within the public school system. The minimum criteria for procedures governing the operation of such educational alternatives shall include the following:

   (a)   the intent of alternative education is to offer students more of a choice about what and how they will learn;

   (b)   the alternatives shall be cooperatively developed by students, teachers and parents;

   (c)   the students enrolled and teachers employed in alternative educational programs shall be selected entirely from volunteers;

   (d)   the alternative must have a well developed and publicized evaluation program; evaluation shall be based upon previously established goals and objectives; evaluation should emphasize the success of alternative ways of developing basic skills;

(e) if the alternative proves to be educationally successful, it should be able to anticipate continuous funding; where funds from outside sources are used, there should be a strong commitment from the local board to continue funding when outside sources are depleted;

(f) the Board of Education and the administration should be firmly committed to the concept of alternatives and be willing to make changes in personnel and policies in order to ensure the success of the program;

(g) sufficient time for planning and inservice training for individual teachers, teams of teachers, and the faculty as a whole must be provided;

(h) involvement of the major teacher organization should be provided for.

The leadership assumed by the California Teachers Association on alternative school is extremely significant. First of all, as a major teachers' organization their actions will be noted nationally. Further they have created a professional climate in which teachers can consider the idea of alternatives and can as individual teachers assume active roles in their implementation. The key point here is that the California Teachers Association has, in essence, said to their member teachers—we as your professional association believe that alternative education makes sense. Alternatives means pluralism in our public schools. Pluralism means that each teacher as a professional is capable of deciding for himself which alternative—if any—makes sense for him.

This means that if the California Teachers Association moves forward on this plan it will have created a new conceptual model for organized teachers—unity with diversity. The teachers are united through the California Teachers Association without compromising the individuality of the teacher and his ability to make independent judgments.

The temptation for teacher organizations to centralize authority, to encourage uniformity among the rank and file has been averted.

It is the present framework of public education that results in one, rather standard, monolithic approach to achieving common educational aims that must be altered. By and large, alternatives are available to the consumer—parents and students—only outside the public school framework in private or parochial schools. Occasionally, by chance, some choice does exist within the public school pattern. This latter point requires some elaboration. The only real alternative inside the standard public school is personal—the strength or sensitivity of a particular teacher or building principal. If a consumer is lucky, he "gets" a good teacher. If the parents decide that they would like their child to be taught by this teacher, they find the "option" quickly discouraged because the present educational ground rules cannot deal adequately with such demands without serious consequences to the normal operation of the school.

Moreover, the student is equally powerless to seek alternatives. He knows that there is only one path—and he must either accept it and adjust to it or perish.

Further, the teacher must accept the standard educational process. What options are there? The teacher is powerless to alter the conventional means of instruction and cannot seek satisfaction in other legitimate educational alternatives unless he chooses to escape to some private school. The fact is that there are many teachers who feel constrained by the present monolithic system and would welcome options that are more congenial to their own styles.

While we are speaking of teachers and other educators, it

might be timely to respond to those critics who view educators as "mediocre." The gist of the critics' complaint is that the more capable people enter other fields such as medicine, law, and government, while the "second string" gravitates toward education. The accusation of mediocrity is often leveled at teachers without considering the institutional environments in which they all too often are forced to function—environments that shape their behavior, constrain their capabilities, and in essence force them into uniformity. Creating optional environments, therefore, could awaken new capacities and talents in educators.

Alternative educational approaches need not take place at different schools; they could be within a single school. For example, if the nongraded "mini-school" becomes an option, then those teachers, parents, and students in the neighborhood school who have chosen this alternative would be free to formulate a "school within a school" concept in which the principles of nongrading are translated into action. Basically, people have a right to the option of their choice. This choice process not only legitimizes an option but succeeds in making the option operational, in making it a behavioral specimen which, in turn, serves to educate other parties of interest. If the nongraded program shows better results than the graded pattern, then more constituents may choose this option; but they will do so because they have been attracted to it instead of having had the option imposed upon them. This process is extremely important in terms of protecting the rights of people in our educational system. At the Parkway School, the "School Without Walls" in Philadelphia, thousands of applications have been submitted to attend the voluntary experiment; masses of students, teachers, and parents have been attracted to the educational concept being tried.

The aim of participation in our society is to promote individual choice. In an open society that values the individual, making choices from among various legitimate options of public education ought to be a right of every individual. In order to promote participation by the individual—whether parent, student, teacher, administrator, or guidance counselor —it is necessary to begin to think differently about our public schools. Let us no longer think of public schooling in all-inclusive terms, with the same kind of education taking place from coast to coast. Instead, let us regard public education as a series of social institutions providing a range of optional educational programs to a diverse population—from a classical academic prep-type school to a community-centered school to a school without walls. Let us think of a public school system that has a common set of educational objectives, objectives aimed toward the values of a democratic society and the maximum growth and development of each individual. Let us also imagine that there are various means to this common set of educational objectives.

In hundreds of schools and school districts, teachers, parents, and students are collaborating to develop a wide range of educational alternatives. This grass-roots approach to reform grows out of the realization that there are other ways of achieving educational goals. They are beginning to realize the restrictions of a structure that expects students and teachers who are different to conform. They now realize that some do, others do not. They now realize that those who do not conform are being penalized; i.e., the school program does not work well for them, but there is nothing wrong with them as learners. They simply learn differently.

Finally, we have realized that instead of having everyone adjust to one pattern of education, why not develop alternatives for those who are not benefiting fully from the standard approach—why not have alternatives that are based on the teaching and learning styles?

For example, in 1970 a group of parents and teachers of the Berkeley Unified School District planned an alternative school which was community-based. Calling themselves Parents and Teachers for Alternatives in Education, this group developed a subschool in which parents teach black studies, native American studies, German, French, anthropology, and humanities. Parents make all important decisions and pay all expenses beyond district obligations. This community school is distinctive in the way its curriculum and teaching utilize the resources of the community.

In other communities, parents and teachers are meeting to develop an alternative elementary classroom that is modeled after the British infant school. This educational approach creates a much more informed classroom structure in which children engage in a variety of activities by choice. The child is encouraged to learn at his own pace. Independence is fostered within each child. The teacher's style is supportive—she helps guide the child.

Some teachers prefer this approach. Some children do also. Instead of having these teachers and students connecting by chance, as is the case at present, why not by choice? Having teachers, students, and parents select the kind of education that best suits their style not only is another fruitful way of individualizing but can avert many of the problems imposed by a uniform system of education.

Is there a parent who has not experienced his child happy with a teacher one year and unhappy another year? Too often, both the teacher and the child are sentenced to each other. Neither has any choice in the matter. Unfortunate mismatches between student and teacher can result in negative attitudes being developed. Students who hate to go to school because of the mismatch are hardly being helped. Instead, if teachers were free to develop alternatives that supported their styles of teaching, then students could choose the style most compatible with their own.

Imagine a neighborhood public school which operated as follows: Parents are cordially invited to a personal conference with school officials several months before the opening of school. Let us assume that the parents are enrolling their child in kindergarten. At the conference, the focus of the discussion is on the child, his interests, concerns, disposition toward learning, etc. The attitude of the school people is one of trying to learn as much as possible about the child. Let us assume further that during the session, the parents reveal that the child is a "middle child," i.e., that he has an older brother and younger sister. The parents begin to speak about the child as being sensitive to competition because at home he is forced to compete with his older brother and more often than not comes out on the short end of things. However, the parents point out the child is alert and able to do many things on his own and loves to build things.

The professional staff is particularly attuned to any indication from the parents of the child's "most natural style of learning." The school people have not only listened to the parents and supported their judgments on the child but they also explain that the parents are also teachers at home. That the home is also a school. That the child has learned many things before coming to school. That the public school and the teacher need to provide continuity between home and school.

At a certain point the school people explain that there are three different but equally valid kindergarten options that the parents can consider for the child. One option is a standard kindergarten which is somewhat competitive in that the children proceed according to established norms; the second option is an informal and non-competitive kindergarten in which the child competes largely with himself, and the third option is Montessori in which the child progresses through a structured sequence.

After talking about each option in greater detail, the parents may spend time observing in each of the three kindergarten classrooms. After the parents are comfortable with their understanding of the three options, they once again sit with school officials to consider the kindergarten best suited for the child.

The professionals have made sure that the parents have had enough information on which to make a choice. Perhaps, as is usually the case, parents will ask the professionals which of the options they feel makes the most sense for the child. The educators may recommend the informal kindergarten, explaining that a "non-competitive" structure may be best for the child given their description of his style at home.

The parents go along with this recommendation but ask what if the child does not respond to the informal classroom? The school people respond that if the informal does not prove to be satisfactory, then we can try "Montessori" and if that does not work we will try the standard—if that is okay with you.

Actually such a scene can be repeated at any level. Naturally, the older the child the more he himself can be brought more directly into the decision-making process. Having the parents and students informed about educational alternatives and providing them with opportunities for genuine choice enhances their sense of control over their own destiny and certainly enhances their satisfaction with the school and the professionals.

Those parents who prefer a more conventional structure

can have it, those who prefer a more contemporary option can have their choice as well.

Furthermore, and this is extremely important, such options are made available only after the school administrators and the teachers have agreed to move in the direction of alternative education and following a decision on the part of *each* teacher to identify her own teaching style. That is to say, *alternative education within public schools begins with the teacher and her most natural style of teaching. Since each teacher has her own style, the creation of a structure which recognizes and legitimizes that style should serve as a liberating force for teachers as well as parents and students.*

There are many teachers who prefer a standard structure and who do well in such classroom environments. There are students and parents who prefer such a style. Under educational alternatives those teachers, parents, and other students have their choice. The standard approach, which is the most common, continues to be a leading option.

Consider also a high school of fifteen hundred students and eighty teachers in Middle America. The school building is new, and most students have aspirations to attend college. There are no signs of any crisis here. The community seems satisfied.

The high school provides each parent, student, and teacher with a choice from among a range of five alternative forms of education. This school-within-a-school arrangement grew out of a co-operative planning process of many months involving teachers, parents, students, and administrators. The five alternative forms of education are:

1. *Traditional School.* The standard pattern is the most familiar. The curriculum is composed of a series of academic courses—English, social studies, science, mathematics, etc. These courses are scheduled in six 55-minute periods. A

teacher specializing in the academic field teaches each course. The basic pattern is one in which there is a more formalized structure for the students and more teacher responsibility for learning.

2. *Flexible School.* In this subschool, the teachers are free to adapt methods of teaching to the styles of the learners. Modular scheduling will be utilized to allow grade flexibility in scheduling. The regular school day has sixteen 20-minute periods. Every Wednesday is "Opportunity Day" in which the student has an option of pursuing his normal schedule or of participating in such activities as college preparation, testing, independent study projects, field trips, community participation and civic responsibility, etc.

3. *PIE School* (Project to Individualize Education). At this school, teaching methods are designed to meet the style of learning of the student. Learning activities usually emerge from regularly scheduled student-teacher planning sessions. Wide use is made of experiences beyond the four walls of the schools. Also the student is encouraged to pursue field experiences, value clarification, communication, and career development. The student is expected to assume responsibility for his own schedule.

4. *Fine Arts School.* This school creates an artistic environment, utilizing the arts as the medium for self- and social development. A comprehensive program of study is offered. In addition to the standard fine arts activities such as music, art, drama, and broadcasting, this school emphasizes the academic disciplines. Tailored courses are also developed, such as opera workshop, non-Western music, playwriting, scenic design and lighting, history of America as seen through the fine arts, and choreography. Emphasis is placed on individual and small group instruction.

5. *Career School.* The thrust of this school is to enable each learner to develop his talents and to relate such talents to his role as worker. In addition to the normal academic subjects, the student spends time in co-ordinated work experiences in the community. The Career Resource Center

in the school enables students to pursue individual concerns, including independent study, tutorial assistance, laboratory work, etc. Graduation from Career School will mean that the student can proceed to a regular four-year college or to a two-year technical junior college.

Each of these schools is housed in one large high school building. There is one over-all school administrator who is still called principal. He supervises Traditional School, with 276 students and 13 teachers; Flexible, with 345 and 14; Project to Individualize Education, 306 and 12; Fine Arts, 130 and 10; Career, 184 and 12. Each subschool has a part-time co-ordinator.

The students indicated their first and second choices on a student preference card after several weeks of orientation to the various alternative schools. A similar process was undertaken with parents.

Since the teachers were viewed as the key to this alternative education program, the faculty of the high school participated fully in the planning. After a first planning period in which the concept of alternative schools was introduced, the faculty voted on whether or not to pursue the idea further. Once accepting the philosophy of options, the teachers and administrators of the school proceeded to plan for a school-within-a-school arrangement. Each of the alternatives finally implemented was developed by the staff. Each teacher had her first choice.

Is this a fictitious school? Not at all. It is now in operation at Quincy Senior High II in Quincy, Illinois. With the help of a Title III planning grant, officials at Quincy developed an "Education by Choice" program at the senior high school.

The interesting aspect of the Quincy Education by Choice plan is that the leadership for the effort was largely professional. Teachers and administrators, together with parents and students, developed alternative education not in response to community pressure, but because the idea made sense educationally. Rather than wait for the educational problems to surface and produce consequent community dissatisfaction, the Quincy team took advantage of their "lead time" to plan for an updated pattern of education for their students.

We have much to learn from the Quincy experience. In addition to exemplary professional leadership and responsibility, the plan was founded on broad-based participation. Federal moneys from the U. S. Office of Education (a Title III grant) were not used to develop more of the same, but became the seed capital for converting the educational process itself.

The Quincy public schools have already begun to point out the advantages to the major parties at interest:

For students: ". . . the opportunity to choose the kind of school they want to attend, necessarily will become more satisfied, motivated, and interested than those students who are coerced into a specific educational institution. Consequently, if a student feels that he is not achieving according to his ability, he may choose to switch to another school that will enable him to better achieve his goals and objectives. Students who are allowed to select a school will also show more pride toward their school, will be more involved in school activities, and will feel more responsible for the success of the school."

For teachers: ". . . meaningful involvement has caused teachers to invest their time and energy in a commitment which will make them feel better about themselves and the things they do. Perhaps for the first time, teachers will own a share of stock in an enterprise that is truly their own. Ownership implies extra effort and dedication to an ever-improving learning system. Their reward will be students, individually and collectively, who sense this commitment and give of themselves to make it work. The implications for learning and student growth in such a system where each participant firmly believes in what he is doing are boundless."

For parents: ". . . stimulate the interest of parents in their child's education. Since parents will be involved in helping their child decide which school to attend, they will need to become more knowledgeable about each school's philosophy and program. Once parents begin to participate directly in the decision-making process concerned with their child's education, they will become more enthusiastic about the school system, have more contact with and want to know more about their child's teachers, and will become more involved in the school program.

The fact that parents will be actively and directly involved in the decisions that affect their child's education, will result in better communication between parents and child, parents and administrators, and parents and teachers. The openness of the proposed system will have a great impact upon the community and the school, because both will be working together in closer harmony than ever before to provide the best education possible. . . ."

For administrators: ". . . The role of building administrators will be modified. Administrators will continue to be supportive of teachers in a logical sense, but will emphasize their role as coordinators and facilitators rather than act as directive and authoritarian personnel. Teachers will perceive their administrators as educational leaders who support a school environment that will allow them freedom to innovate, make decisions, and solve problems in each school-within-a-school situation. This cooperative relationship in planning and implementation will provide administrators with an opportunity for real involvement in the learning process and, as such, will help them feel more satisfied with their role.

In general, the conception of an administrator will shift from all-around educational handyman to that of a coordinator, facilitator, and conciliator of a school environment that will allow teachers and students the freedom and support necessary to maximize individual learning and achievement."[8]

We seem to have learned that there are individual differences among teachers as well as students, that attempts to match teaching-learning styles may be another route to individualization, that expecting a pluralistic society to continue to adjust to a monolithic educational process can only lead to increased frustration for learner, family, and teacher. We have finally learned to offer options within our public schools.

Education by Choice accomplishes a number of significant educational ingredients. It begins to break up the mass-production, factory system of schooling. This internal decentralization means that instead of uniform schools for thousands, there emerge smaller, more intimate schools of between seventy-five and three hundred students. Families of teachers and students are grouped together by mutual consent and common interests. The opportunities of forming "educational communities" whose environment itself becomes a major curriculum for learning are greatly enhanced.

The establishment of smaller learning units takes us a step closer toward the humanization process. Also, important decision-making authority is returned to the individual rather than to his representatives, to individuals closest to the point of action—teachers, students, and parents. Making decisions about the kind of educational process with which one wants to connect can assist in restoring a sense of lost potency to these central parties at interest.

[8] From *Education by Choice*, Application for Operational Grant under Elementary and Secondary Education Act, Public Law 89-10, Title III, submitted by Quincy Public Schools, District 172, Quincy, Illinois, pp. 17–20.

One of the reasons for Quincy's successful launching of
Education by Choice has to do with the careful application
of certain ground rules that helped legitimize the plan within
public schools:

The first concerns the common sets of objectives toward
which each alternative is directed. That is to say, there were
common and comprehensive educational ends: basic skills,
academic achievement, talent development, preparation for
societal roles (citizen, worker, consumer, etc.), development
of personal identity—which every alternative had to achieve
in its own distinctive way. Without this common set of des-
tinations, each option could have selected its own objectives.
But public schools are responsible for a broad range of goals.
Without such accountability, any educational alternative
could be considered legitimate, even those that had a limited
set of objectives or those that did not bother to consider
objectives at all. Alternative public education means diversi-
fying the means to common ends.

The second ground rule establishes alternative schools as a
nonexclusive enterprise. That is to say, no educational option
can be considered legitimate if it practices exclusivity in any
form—racial, social, sexual, religious, etc. Alternatives should
have a coherent philosophy of education dedicated unwaver-
ingly to the growth and development of *each* learner.

A third principle establishes each alternative being implemented as equally valid. An alternative cannot make exaggerated claims by belittling another alternative. Such delibera-
tions only lead to ill feelings among professionals and laymen
alike, threatening the co-operative spirit of alternative education.

A fourth ground rule deals with the process of change itself. Unless alternatives are based on *individual* choice, then

this pattern cannot work. Each parent, student, and teacher must be given the right to choose the alternative that is most compatible. No alternative should be imposed on any parent, teacher, or student. The process of change is by attraction, not imposition.

A fifth rule concerns evaluation. Each alternative must be willing to be evaluated. Since each alternative is moving toward the same ends, it becomes necessary to assess how the process is doing. The purposes of evaluation are twofold: to use evaluation information as a basis for continuing to improve the alternative and to help determine the relative effectiveness of each option.

Since evaluation procedures are complex, a number of methods should be employed, including parent, student, and teacher satisfaction and anthropological and sociological participant-observer techniques.

Finally, alternative education should not depend on increases in per-student expenditures. Each alternative would adjust to the going per-pupil expenditure rate that happens to be in the school district. The idea is to use existing resources (human and material) more effectively, through alternative schools.

This does not mean that (1) seed or planning money is not needed or (2) that the existing per-student expenditure rate is appropriate. The point is that to base alternative education on an increase in school expenditures is to place the plan in jeopardy before it can get off the ground.

The strength of alternative education is that it provides existing teachers, parents, and students—who are already enrolled and for whom resources already exist—with options. Consequently, teachers who are being paid but who are spending their time and effort in one way will, under alternative schools, be able to use their style and talents differently.

This is more of a rearrangement, a realignment, of existing resources than it is an add-on effort.

Catching on to the possibilities of developing other ways of educating a pluralistic student body, many teachers, parents, and students have begun to plan and implement alternative public schools. Teachers and administrators are swarming to workshops on open education. Hundreds of open classrooms have sprung up across the nation. (For instance, half the public schools in the state of North Dakota are considered to have open education.) Dozens of cities have begun their own versions of a school without walls.

These new alternatives differ sharply from the options traditionally available in public schools, such as vocational and special education, schools for dropouts and unwed mothers—tracks that carried with them a psychological classification that was negative when compared to those in the academic track. Moreover, these options were based more on chance than choice.

Before the alternatives movement, the child was assigned to a teacher whose teaching style may or may not have been congruent with the child's learning style. Some students responded, others did not, but neither teacher nor child had any choice in the matter.

Alternatives provide new opportunities for a match in teaching and learning styles.[9] Choice lets students select programs that best fit them. Parents, who have played key roles as teachers at home, are in a good position to help select the alternative that best suits their child's distinctive pattern for learning. Similarly teachers can select the alternative that best supports their temperament and approach.

[9] For a discussion of matching teaching and learning styles see Mario Fantini, *Public Schools of Choice*, Simon and Schuster, Chapter III.

On a national basis, public school alternatives fall into several categories:

Classroom alternatives. Some alternatives are found at the classroom level of neighborhood schools. For instance, a first-grade teacher who favors open education may be the only one of three or four teachers who does. Hence she offers an option to any first-grade parents who wish an open classroom. The same principle applies at any grade level and with any legitimate educational pattern. A teacher may offer, for example, a Montessori, behavior modification, or a multiculture alternative classroom.

Alternative classrooms have certain advantages. They start slowly. Parents and students are introduced to options gradually and within the confines of their own neighborhood school. No one is forced to participate, and even if no overwhelming dissatisfaction with the school exists, alternative classrooms provide a choice to those parents or teachers who are dissatisfied.

Schools within schools. Another manifestation of alternative education is the idea of schools within schools, or mini-schools within a formerly unitary school. Any neighborhood elementary, junior or middle, or high school can become two or more smaller schools, each school emphasizing a distinctive pattern of education. Each subschool is made available to students, parents, and teacher by choice. There are many such schools, both urban and suburban, in various stages of development. Examples are:

Haaren High School in New York City has a mini-school arrangement. This boys' school is organized into a complex of fourteen mini-schools within a single building. Each mini-school has its own co-ordinator (who is responsible to the principal), five teachers, one street worker, and from 125 to 150 students.

Walt Whitman High School in Montgomery County, Maryland, a middle-class suburb, was one of the first to consider schools within schools similar to that of Haaren.

As we have described earlier, after comprehensive planning,

the high school in Qunicy, Illinois, is now developing subschool alternatives. With extensive faculty, student, and community participation, a range of alternatives were sketched. The
Education by Choice planning team proposed seven options,
in terms of learning environments, as follows: (1) primarily
teacher-directed; (2) direction from both teacher and student,
but for the most part teacher-directed; (3) students and teachers
together plan the experiences for the participants; (4) primary
focus on considering the various areas of learning in relation
to the arts; (5) primary focus on career orientation and preparation; (6) learning environment for special education students; and (7) learning environment for dropout-prone students.

Schools within established schools have certain advantages:
(1) they are convenient for parents, students, and teachers;
(2) they provide opportunities for staff and community to
participate in the development of alternatives; and (3) by
using the facilities of an established school, they can make
fuller use of existing resources such as physical education, music,
and art facilities and counselors.

The disadvantages are the problems that arise when any established social system is disturbed. There may be serious resistance
by those who perceive alternatives as a threat to existing arrangements.

Separate alternative schools. A popular mode for alternative education is the development of a new public school in a
facility separate from existing schools. The Village School in
Great Neck, New York, is housed in a church basement. An
abandoned missile base in Long Beach, New York, houses the
Nike School. The Brown School in Louisville, Kentucky, uses
a downtown office building for its location. Such descriptions
are repeated across the country:

The St. Paul Open School is actually a three-story former
factory building now brightly decorated. This alternative school
does not mandate attendance. Each student pursues his own
tailored plan. The major learning areas—humanities, math,
science, and industrial arts—make up the organization. Teachers
serve as learning facilitators. The classrooms have an informal,

family-type flavor to them (armchairs, sofas, tables, lamps, and so forth).

The Murray Road Alternative School in Newton, Massachusetts, is located in a former elementary school and has about 115 college-bound high school students and eight teachers who participate in an informal educational community. With only British and American history required, there is great freedom to pursue individual interests and concerns.

Separate alternative schools have advantages. For one thing, they can start from scratch. Away from traditional constraints, they are free to mold new concepts of teaching and learning with sympathetic participants. However, disadvantages may arise if a separate alternative school becomes the only experiment in optional education, thus leaving out other parents, teachers, and students.

Systems of alternative schools. Several school systems have attempted to transform significant portions of their districts into alternative school patterns. For example, the Berkeley Unified School District in California has generated twenty-four distinct alternative schools. Such alternatives fall into four broad patterns:

1. *Multiculture schools.* These schools include children carefully selected on the basis of diversity of race, socioeconomic status, age, and sex. During part of the school day the students meet and work together. At other times they meet in their own ethnic, social, or educational groups, learning their own culture, language customs, history and heritage, or other special curriculum; later, these aspects are shared with the wider group.

2. *Community schools.* The organization, curriculum, and teaching approach of these schools come from outside the classroom—from the community. There may well be total parent involvement, with both the school day and week being extended into shared family life. There will be use of courts, markets, museums, parks, theaters, and other educational resources in the community.

3. *Structured skills training schools.* These schools are graded

and emphasize the learning of basic skills—reading, writing, and math. Learning takes place primarily in the classroom and is directed by either one teacher or a team of teachers working together.

4. *Schools without walls.* The focus of these schools is the child and his development. The staff deals with the child rather than the subject. The schools are ungraded, and typically their style and arrangements are unstructured. Their goals are to have the students grow in self-understanding and self-esteem, to learn how to cope with social and intellectual frustration, and to master the basic and social skills through their own interests.

The school district of Philadelphia has a director of alternative programs who is co-ordinating the development of more than fifty alternative learning environments. These are modeled after open classrooms, schools without walls, and mini-schools, and include schools for students with special problems, such as gifted learners, academic failures, and disruptive and pregnant students.

The Minneapolis public schools have initiated a Southeast Alternatives Program serving all students in that area of the city. Elementary students can attend any of the following four types of schools:

1. A contemporary school, Tuttle, which offers curriculum innovations but maintains a teacher-directed, structured curriculum and grade-level school organization.

2. A continuous progress school, a part of Pratt and Motely Schools, in which each child advances at his own pace without regard to grade level and in which instruction is by teams and based on a carefully sequenced curriculum in basic skills.

3. An open school, Marcy, which combines flexible curriculum, scheduling, and age grouping in the style of the British infant schools. Children take a great deal of initiative for their own education, with the emphasis on pursuing their own interests.

4. A free school, the Minneapolis Free School, which extends through the twelfth grade. Students, parents, volunteers, and faculty develop the courses, and much off-campus experience is included. The initial enrollment of 70 students was expanded to 150 during 1972–73, and, according to school officials, a more structured, content-oriented program will be developed.

It should be clear by now that, educationally speaking, alternatives run the entire gamut from student-directed to teacher-directed. On the one end, there are alternatives that accord the learner considerable freedom to determine how he will learn, what he will learn, when, where, and with whom. On the other end, these elements are predetermined by the school itself. In between, there is a vast range of possibilities. With such a perspective, we can see the over-all pattern into which are fitted free schools, open classrooms, ungraded schools, schools without walls, prep schools, and so forth.

A few words on the politics of the alternative schools movement are always appropriate. We have learned that any change involves politics. Alternative education as a change is significantly different from many other reform plans in that it is based on choice and is, therefore, voluntary. It is chosen by teachers, parents, and students by attraction; it is not superimposed. The "something for everybody" flavor of alternatives reduces the inevitable political conflict that results when people have no choice in the reform proposal being implemented.

Once again we must underscore that no real reform can be achieved without the support of the frontline agents—teachers, parents, and students. Alternatives are grass roots oriented and cater to these three basic publics. The role of the school administrator is to provide an enabling structure. This means giving basic information on alternatives to interested parties and arranging and facilitating meetings among teachers, parents, and students.

Alternatives often run into resistance when they make exaggerated claims following a negative diagnosis of the standard process in the public schools. Such behavior by advocates of alternative schools only solicits resistance. First, the "blasting" of what exists makes those associated with standard education feel inferior, a mood hardly conducive to co-operation. Second, projecting high expectations of the proposed alternatives serves both to increase the resentment of those in the standard process and to plant the seeds of frustration for those participating in the alternative itself. No one alternative can do it all.

Alternatives are in operation in Great Neck, New York; Newton, Massachusetts; Webster Groves, Missouri; New Haven and Hartford, Connecticut; and New York City, as well as hundreds of other places. The National Consortium for Options in Public Education at Indiana University estimates that alternative public schools exist in thirty-five states.[10]

In Ann Arbor a team of six teachers from diverse backgrounds initiated the planning for an alternative high school. In the spring of 1972, after participation of students, parents, and other residents in the development of the plan, a new alternative secondary school, Community High School, was created. A brochure, describing the Community High School, includes the strong sense of co-operation among the basic parties.

The Planning Committee is grateful to the staff of the Ann Arbor Public Schools and to the students, parents and residents of the Ann Arbor Community for their enthusiasm, support

[10] Changing Schools No. 008 Director of Alternative Public Schools.

and participation in the new program and to the community resources, who have agreed to join the school staff in providing a core of exciting experiences for Ann Arbor youth.

An integral part of the operation of the alternative school is parent involvement.

Community High School is organized into four houses; each house is composed of six forums, the Parent Support Group, and Educational Assistants.

Parent Support Groups join with students and staff to evaluate programs, teach interest groups, suggest new raw resources, and work with school activities and projects.

Educational Assistants teach courses on a part-time basis when teachers are unable to increase their workload or lack expertise in an area.[11]

In Spring Valley, New York, over a hundred parents formed an organization, Parents for Alternative Public Education for Ramapo. Their interest was in developing educational options within the elementary and secondary schools in their district. This group of parents became quite active. They attended board of education meetings, held sessions with school administrators and teachers, contacted nearby colleges, etc. Their efforts led to the co-operative development of alternative education in their schools. In Los Angeles, California, a group of parents, with the support of Women For, an active civic organization, helped establish alternative public schools in that city.

The alternative education movement provides parents, teachers, and students with opportunities to collaborate on common concerns. For instance, in the town of Sharon, Massachusetts, a group of parents, teachers, and students came together for the purpose of exploring an alternative school within their public school system.

[11] Unpublished Blueprint of Community High School, Ann Arbor, Michigan, Public Schools, Spring 1972.

They came together on a common goal to humanize education. They developed an idea for a school in which learning would be emphasized rather than teaching, where the program would fit the child rather than the other way around, where co-operation replaced competition, where the school would reflect a democratic rather than authoritarian climate.

At the present time, they are preparing a proposal to be submitted to the School Committee. The fact that parents, teachers, and students worked together in this effort should increase significantly the chance for Sharon to have an alternative school in the near future.

Among the most urgently needed reforms is a strong commitment for teachers to change. This means getting involved with the process. This process, if it is also to be linked to parents and students, cannot take place according to ground rules and by teachers. They need to demonstrate their genuine interest in the welfare of the children by devoting time and energy to the task of reform. Reform is not a 9:00 A.M. to 3:00 P.M. proposition.

During this period of public accounting, teachers displaying this uniform union stance are viewed as being selfish—concerned with their own welfare rather than that of the children and society. Such a position can only lead to conflict.

All this has come about with some help from the Ford Foundation and the Experimental Schools Program of the U. S. Office of Education.

Alternative schools provide some plausible answer to the current mood of public accountability. Certainly, we have indicated that alternative schools provide dissatisfied educational consumers with options. This may make some dent on the problem of consumer satisfaction.

Probably equally, if not more, important is that alternative education need not cost more money. To an overtaxed citizen, this approach to reform will have particular appeal. In the past, school reform proposals have invariably cost more money. As we have suggested, alternative education is based on a *reutilization of existing resources*. This plan wants to use what we already have, differently, more effectively. For instance, there are teachers on current payrolls who feel that their style of teaching could be enhanced if they were able to create an alternative school. Since these teachers are already being paid—since the parents and students who would select this alternative are also connected with the current schools—the problem is more rearrangement than added costs. Current school budgets carry items for supplies and materials, in-service education, maintenance, etc. Alternate schools simply use these sources differently.

To be sure, there may be additional costs, e.g., rental of space, but in these cases, the school district can usually transfer funds from one line item to another. In some cases, the parents, teachers, and students are so motivated by the alternative that they assume the responsibilities for additional costs themselves.

In other cases, alternatives can actually save money for the school district. For instance, a school without walls can save taxpayers the cost of new expensive buildings. Since in this type of option the community is used as classroom—e.g., newspaper reporters teach writing to students in their own offices, and museums, theaters, hospitals, insurance companies, etc., use their own settings for instruction—the construction cost savings could run as high as fifteen million dollars.

As we have suggested, funding sources can also be tapped. The fiscal rationale for alternative education is one of conversion—we need small amounts of capital to convert from one uniform system of public education to flexible, optional framework. This concept of conversion capital connects with the intent of much of the federal legislation in education.

The fundamental approach of alternative education is that it is based on *individual* choice. Individual parents, students, and teachers *choose* the form of education that best suits his style. As an individual choice plan, it breaks from the centralized, collective format that presently governs our schools. Connections among teachers, parents, and students are made in terms of a common attraction—the educational alternative. Because teacher style is more nearly matched with learner style, clashes between the two are minimized. Also, many of these options will be developed by teachers, students, and parents working together. Such co-operation leads to mutual understanding and trust which may transcend collective interests.

The appeal here is to the teacher as professional—a professional with a strong commitment to the child. As an individual and as a member of a teachers' organization, the individual teacher now alone can help establish this professionalism for the American teacher. Committed teachers can influence the direction of professional associations to support and lead the movement for reform of a system that is as restrictive to the profession as it is to the consumer.

Developing optional learning environments within public schools, therefore, can provide teachers and other educators with new opportunities to exercise their professional talents and skills. As professionals with expertise, teachers are the major designers and implementers of educational alternatives. Without teachers and their pedagogical knowledge few legitimate and lasting alternatives can be mounted. Whether formal or informal, competitive or non-competitive learning environments are planned. The expertise of professionals is required. Teacher judgments are crucial to the task of developing valued options. Further, teachers themselves will have to "deliver" the alternatives to students and parents.

Consequently, the offering alternatives will require the fullest utilization of professional know-how.

This liberation of teacher talent is at the heart of being professional. It requires the individuality of the teacher, his distinctive style and accumulated wisdom. Freeing the teacher professionally is essential to the unfolding of alternative public schools.

By recognizing the individual teacher, the school structure legitimizes diversity and breaks the stranglehold of uniformity.

Alternative education reforms public schools without destroying them, without denying the rights of the basic parties at interest. No alternative is imposed. It is based on choice. Further, since the standard alternative remains, this plan does not threaten the majority of teachers, parents, and students who prefer this educational approach. Since most of us have been oriented to the standard, it will probably be the alternative most demanded.

No alternative is given a better over-all rating than any other. Each alternative must be legitimate. As such, each option is aimed at the same ends. They are different roads to the same destination. The participants simply choose the best road for them.

The process of change is based on *attraction* rather than *imposition*. This feature is crucial. In the past, most reform efforts have been based either on majority rule or on administrative preference. Under these conditions, a significant portion of students, parents, and teachers fell victim to programs by imposition. At the present time, there are programs, e.g., modular scheduling and open education, that are being implemented without choice. Several decades ago, some pro-

fessionals imposed "progressive education" on some schools
—only to have a rebellion occur in the community.

The point is that what is a good educational idea to some
is not to others. Since there are different ways to deal with
the same goals, imposing one plan on everybody is politically
and educationally vulnerable. Conflicts pull people apart and
require the use of time and effort to heal the wounds. These
same energies could be used to update the schools themselves.

Since the public schools have become political targets, with
special interests motivating each "power group," it is dangerous to consider change through imposition. Such a strategy
too often results in further polarization and conflict—which
does little in the way of dealing with the fundamental problem of generating a new effectiveness in learning.

Rather, we need a new strategy for change based on attraction and choice. The political realities in our schools
necessitate an approach to change which gives something to
everybody, especially the frontline agents—teachers, students,
and parents. Those teachers, parents, and students who prefer the kind of program they now have can keep it. However,
those who prefer an alternative to the standard program have
a right to such an option. Thus, in any school, if a group of
teachers, parents, and students prefer a multi-cultural approach to education or a prep mini-school to flourish—that
should be their choice—as long as it is legitimate, i.e., adheres
to the ground rules for participation in an education by
choice plan.

We must underscore the importance of individual choice.
In a framework of educational options, individual teachers,
individual students, individual parents, are making decisions.
Each is being given the power and responsibility to choose the
kind of education he prefers. This approach to decision-mak-

ing begins to transfer important power from some centralized group to the individual. On something as personally important as education, the individual's right to choice must be enhanced.

Our present form of school governance is based on so-called representative democracy—that is to say, when an elected or selected group makes decisions for the masses on the grounds that they represent the interests and concerns of those each represents. School boards, whether central or regional, are based on this concept.

However, given the stage of individual concern for the quality of education, such representative bodies are limited in their capacity to be responsive.

The alternate schools plan retains a representative body to maintain over-all policies, but delegates to the individual the right to choose from among legitimate educational alternatives.

Centralized agents such as school boards, superintendents, and teachers' organizations are crucial in creating the enabling structure for this individual education-by-choice model. Since much power rests with these central agents, they are the ones who will have to assume leadership in generating a new educational framework in which they can transfer decision-making authority to the individual student, parent, and teacher.

Without this alternative schools framework for our public schools, the politics of power will continue to display itself through confrontation. The will of one group will be imposed on the other, resulting in further hostility and struggle. Schools swimming in such seas cannot long survive—nor can the children themselves, as they increasingly fall victim to the politics of negative power.

While educational alternatives are no panacea for the long years of neglect, they do represent one of the few proposals that are both politically and educationally viable.

Our experience to date with the infant alternative public school movement has taught us to re-emphasize rules that need to be applied to minimize problems and to guide the legitimization process. We summarize these again briefly:

1. Alternatives are not superimposed, but a matter of choice for all participants—teachers, parents, and students.

2. Alternatives are viewed as another way of providing education alongside the existing pattern, which continues to be legitimate. Alternatives are different from special programs for dropouts, unwed mothers, and the like.

3. Alternatives do not practice exclusivity.

4. Alternatives do not make exaggerated claims of accomplishments that may be deceptive in the long run.

5. Alternatives are aimed at a broad, common set of educational objectives, not just limited objectives. Alternative public schools are responsible to the public for comprehensive cognitive and affective goals that cannot be compromised, including basic skills, learning to learn skills, talent development, socialization of basic societal roles (citizen, consumer, worker), self-concept development.

6. Alternatives do not cost more money than existing per-student expenditures.

7. Alternatives need to be evaluated.

During the remainder of this decade, we should see an expansion of alternative education. What can result is a gradual expansion of the framework of public education to include many former alternative private schools. Over time, we could emerge with a redefined system of public education that is diverse, self-renewing, and responsive to a pluralistic society.

However, we should all take note of another possible path to school improvement, one in which the majority will dictate the type of education for all—education by majority rule. And the kind of education demanded will be what citizens have known best—a return to a uniform 3 Rs approach.

Unfortunately, we are also in a period in which both strains of tomorrow's education have their beginnings today. One path leads to a reforming of public education through alternatives, co-operatively developed by teachers, parents, and students. This has been the path suggested in this book. However, the other path, with an equally good chance of emerging as the dominant form of public education, is toward increased restrictiveness and uniformity imposed by state legislation responding to public pressure. As the public concern increases for the quality of the schools, so will public demands for results. Already, we have witnessed the use of standardized scores as a basis for revealing shortcomings in the standard school approach. As we have suggested, most parents and other taxpayers are products of schools that were uniform and regimented. They have come to believe that the only good school is one which is rigid, which is strict, which gives homework, tests, etc. In the absence of a massive program of public education that would provide other sensible ways of looking at reform, this internalized notion of what constitutes good schooling will be demanded increasingly because the public will want what it knows best. This can mean a more rigid process of schooling—one in which the student who does not adjust is treated in the same way we treat losers. In fact, we have already witnessed school systems unable to meet the demands of a diverse student population degenerate into "blackboard jungles." We have already witnessed student protests, the dropout rate in cities is still high, the absentee role is increasing.

Generally there is a perception that too much permissiveness is being tolerated by schoolmen. What is needed is a return to "law and order" in the schools. It makes a lot of sense to restore order in schools that appear to be chaotic. Students for whom the school is working are disturbed by the unfavorable school climate. Parents of these students raise concerns. Many move out to different areas where the school reflects a more homogeneous, middle-class flavor. Certainly when the schools are viewed as in a state of disorder, it makes good sense to demand order. But as we have suggested, it is difficult to have all students adjust to one approach to education. Teachers cannot keep order on their own; principals find it increasingly difficult to maintain a "tight ship." The incidents of teacher attacks by students is rising at an alarming rate. Teachers need to be protected; discipline needs to be restored by force, if necessary. Consequently, teachers' unions are beginning to negotiate for police guards in the schools. Thus, we hear of so many such guards being hired per so many students. Ironically, a decade ago educators were asking for a school guidance counselor per so many students. Now the demands are for policemen—what will be the need tomorrow?

Obviously such a trend will support a more restrictive educational approach. This is the "no-nonsense" approach. Even those who would not want such a repressive system would support greater standardization. These persons would point to the low test scores in basic skills as measured by standardized tests. But standardized tests have been developed to support a standardized, uniform pattern of education. Therefore, by demanding accountability through test results, they, too, push the schools into a box of uniformity.

The danger exists, therefore, that we can end up with a more monolithic, hierarchical, regimented system of public education than the one we now have. We are seeing a steady return to human classification based on I.Q., non-promotion policies, proposals for lowering the compulsory attendance age. These are regressive movements if they are imposed on everyone. The results of such a monolithic trend will, in the long run, be negative to the growth and development interest of learners. The psychology of individual differences runs counter to uniformity. We can end up with the fundamental irony of an autocratic education institution, trying to engender democratic values to the next generation.

Hopefully, this present demand for public accountability, together with the leadership of educators interested in reform, can generate enough movement with options in education to provide an alternative to the repressive path to school improvement. If enough people are exposed to the legitimacy of options, then the more democratic approach to school improvement, through educational diversity and choice, can gain national support.

The choice is now clearly in the hands of those who have the power—including teachers' associations. Will they continue to play by the old political power game that can only lead to violent collision, or will they lead in creating a ball game in which the individual teacher, parent, and student become the major co-operating players? We appear to be at a fork in the road—one leading to collision, the other to co-operation.

Teachers' unions especially are at this proverbial crossroads; they can continue to provide leadership that seeks increased power used to solidify teachers and separate them from the public, or they can encourage teachers to work with parents and students at the individual school levels to develop educational alternatives based on choice.

It should be clear by now that no one is advocating that teachers not have professional organizations. Obviously, professional organizations have an immensely important role to perform in contemporary society. We are in an age of education. Half the citizens of our country are involved in educational activities. We need an educated citizenry to make democracy function effectively. All societal roles have their roots in our educational institutions.

We desperately need professional organizations which help establish public policies that promote educational opportunities for the positive development of each person. They protect the noblest values of an open society: dignity of the person, compassion, social justice, and the host of other standards by which we judge the worth of a democracy. Since educational forces extend beyond the boundaries of public schools (e.g. media, the home), policy-makers need informed guidance in creating conditions that support the growth of the individual. Professional organizations can assume a leadership role in providing such guidance.

Professional organizations can also assist in conducting basic research and evaluation that search out those conditions that promote learning. Of crucial importance is the need for such organizations to mount a strong program of educating the public to the many facets of improving the learning environments of children and youth. Professional organizations can also continue to deal with the so-called bread and butter concerns of teachers—salary and working conditions.

It is when professional organizations assume roles that deprive parents and other citizens and individual teachers of their rights that they overlap the legitimate limits of their responsibility.

But above all we need professional organizations and the cumulative integrity of their individual members to help us through a profound period of public school reform. The proverbial crossroads are now before us. The moment is urgent.

For one road, in our opinion, leads to increased collision—the other to increased co-operation and progressive school reform. One road will be disastrous for the public schools, the students, and the teaching profession itself. The other gives some hope of remaking our public schools and our teaching profession through a process of co-operation.

Our sense is that we have a majority of teachers wanting to assume a professional role that commits them fully to the humanistic growth of each learner. This majority desperately wants to do the right thing. They would gladly embrace an alternative schools philosophy of reform and participate actively in its implementation. This group needs to be reached soon if we are to revitalize the public schools and the teaching profession itself.

On the other hand, without feasible plans for reform the negative forces described in the previous pages will serve to increase teacher militancy in the direction of self-preservation and away from the developmental needs of the learner. Unfortunately, it appears that those who now lead teachers seem to be preoccupied with the latter. It is time they reorder the priorities of their organizations in favor of children and to the reforms that are necessary to provide quality education for each learner. In this spirit, we offer our plan for alternative education.

The final choice is not only in the hands of teachers' unions, or school boards, or superintendents, but with all people of good will. Most Americans will be involved in the road we ultimately take. May we have the time and wisdom to choose wisely!